TORN COUNTRY:

TURKEY

between Secularism *and* Islamism

HERBERT AND JANE DWIGHT WORKING GROUP ON ISLAMISM AND THE INTERNATIONAL ORDER

TORN COUNTRY:

TURKEY

between Secularism *and* Islamism

Zeyno Baran

HOOVER INSTITUTION PRESS
Stanford University   *Stanford, California*

www.hoover.org

Hoover Institution Press Publication No. 590

Hoover Institution at Leland Stanford Junior University, Stanford, California, 94305-6010

First printing 2010
16 15 14 13 12 11 10   9 8 7 6 5 4 3 2 1

Manufactured in the United States of America

The paper used in this publication meets the minimum Requirements of the American National Standard for Information Sciences—Permanence of Paper for Printed Library Materials, ANSI/NISO Z39.48–1992. ♾

Library of Congress Cataloging-in-Publication Data
Torn country: Turkey between secularism and Islamism
By Zeyno Baran
    p.   cm.—(Hoover Institution Press publication series ; 590)
Includes bibliographical references and index.
ISBN 978-0-8179-1144-7 (cloth : alk. paper)
ISBN 978-0-8179-1146-1 (e-book)
1. AK Parti (Turkey)   2. Turkey—Politics and government—1980–
3. Islam and politics—Turkey.   4. Islam and secularism—Turkey.
I. Title.
JQ1809.A8A433   2010
324.2561′04—dc22   201020765

The Hoover Institution gratefully acknowledges
the following individuals and foundations
for their significant support of the

HERBERT AND JANE DWIGHT WORKING GROUP
ON ISLAMISM AND THE INTERNATIONAL ORDER

Herbert and Jane Dwight
Stephen Bechtel Foundation
Lynde and Harry Bradley Foundation
Mr. and Mrs. Clayton W. Frye Jr.
Lakeside Foundation

CONTENTS

FOREWORD

For decades, the themes of the Hoover Institution have revolved around the broad concerns of political and economic and individual freedom. The Cold War that engaged and challenged our nation during the twentieth century guided a good deal of Hoover's work, including its archival accumulation and research studies. The steady output of work on the communist world offers durable testimonies to that time, and struggle. But there is no repose from history's exertions, and no sooner had communism left the stage of history than a huge challenge arose across the broad lands of the Islamic world. A brief respite, and a meandering road, led from the fall of the Berlin Wall on 11/9 in 1989 to 9/11. Hoover's newly launched project, the Herbert and Jane Dwight Working Group on Islamism and the International Order, is our contribution to a deeper understanding of the struggle in the Islamic world between order and its nemesis, between Muslims keen to protect the rule of reason and the gains of modernity, and those determined to deny the Islamic world its place in the modern international order of states. The United States is deeply engaged, and dangerously exposed, in the Islamic world, and we see our working group as part and parcel of the ongoing confrontation with the radical Islamists who have declared war on the states in their midst, on American power and interests, and on the very order of the international state system.

The Islamists are doubtless a minority in the world of Islam. But they are a determined breed. Their world is the Islamic emirate, led by self-styled "emirs and mujahedeen in the path of God" and legitimized by the pursuit of the caliphate that collapsed with the end of the Ottoman Empire in 1924. These masters of terror and their foot soldiers have made it increasingly difficult to integrate the world of Islam into modernity. In the best of worlds, the entry of Muslims into modern culture and economics would have presented difficulties of no small consequence: the strictures on women, the legacy of humiliation and self-pity, the outdated educational systems, and an explosive demography that is forever at war with social and economic gains. But the borders these warriors of the faith have erected between Islam and "the other" are particularly forbidding. The lands of Islam were the lands of a crossroads civilization, trading routes and mixed populations. The Islamists have waged war, and a brutally effective one it has to be conceded, against that civilizational inheritance. The leap into the modern world economy, as attained by China and India in recent years, will be virtually impossible in a culture that feeds off belligerent self-pity, and endlessly calls for wars of faith.

The war of ideas with radical Islamism is inescapably central to this Hoover endeavor. The strategic context of this clash, the landscape of that Greater Middle East, is the other pillar. We face three layers of danger in the heartland of the Islamic world: states that have succumbed to the sway of terrorists in which state authority no longer exists (Afghanistan, Somalia, and Yemen), dictatorial regimes that suppress their people at home and pursue deadly weapons of mass destruction and adventurism abroad (Iraq under Saddam Hussein, the Iranian theocracy), and "enabler" regimes, such as the ones in Egypt and Saudi Arabia, which export their own problems with radical Islamism to other parts of the Islamic world and beyond. In this context, the task of reversing Islamist radicalism and of reforming and strengthening the state across the entire Muslim world—the Middle East, Africa, as well as South, Southeast, and Central Asia—is the greatest strategic challenge of the twenty-first century. The essential starting point is detailed knowledge of our enemy.

Thus, the working group will draw on the intellectual resources of Hoover and Stanford and on an array of scholars and practitioners from elsewhere in the United States, the Middle East, and the broader world of Islam. The scholarship on contemporary Islam can now be read with discernment. A good deal of it, produced in the immediate aftermath of 9/11, was not particularly deep and did not stand the test of time and events. We, however, are in the favorable position of a "second generation" assessment of that Islamic material. Our scholars and experts can report, in a detailed, authoritative way, on Islam within the Arabian Peninsula, on trends within Egyptian Islam, on the struggle between the Kemalist secular tradition in Turkey and the new Islamists, particularly on the fight for the loyalty of European Islam between those who accept the canon and the discipline of modernism and those who don't.

Arabs and Muslims need not be believers in American exceptionalism, but our hope is to engage them in this contest of ideas. We will not necessarily aim at producing primary scholarship, but such scholarship may materialize in that our participants are researchers who know their subjects intimately. We see our critical output as essays accessible to a broader audience, primers about matters that require explication, op-eds, writings that will become part of the public debate, and short, engaging books that can illuminate the choices and the struggles in modern Islam.

We see this endeavor as a faithful reflection of the values that animate a decent, moderate society. We know the travails of modern Islam, and this working group will be unsparing in depicting them. But we also know that the battle for modern Islam is not yet lost, that there are brave men and women fighting to retrieve their faith from the extremists. Some of our participants will themselves be intellectuals and public figures who have stood up to the pressure. The working group will be unapologetic about America's role in the Muslim world. A power that laid to waste religious tyranny in Afghanistan and despotism in Iraq, that came to the rescue of the Muslims in the Balkans when they appeared all but doomed, has given much to those burdened populations. We haven't always understood Islam and Muslims—hence this inquiry. However, it is a given of the working group that the pursuit of modernity and human welfare, and of the rule of law and reason, in Islamic lands is the common ground between America and contemporary Islam.

IF THE THEOCRATIC REPUBLIC IN IRAN is one bookend of the Islamic political experience, Turkey is the other, the quintessential secular and modernist polity in the Islamic world. There is an overworked image of Turkey as the "bridge" between Islam and the West, a country across the divide between Europe and the lands of Islam. But that image of Turkey has led observers, Turks, and outsiders astray.

In this study of Turkey, Zeyno Baran, a scholar of Turkish birth and an American education (at Stanford), delivers an authoritative reading of the changes that have settled on Turkey, and that country's struggle over its identity between the secularists—dubbed the Kemalists, after the legendary founder Mustafa Kemal Atatürk—and the Islamists who came forth to challenge his vision, meeting with increasing success in the last decade or so. Baran, at home with Turkey's language, culture, and history, situates this contest in an age-old Turkish quest for a place in the modern society of nations. In the early 1990s, when Turkish secularism seemed ascendant, Samuel P. Huntington, the late Harvard political scientist, described Turkey as a "torn country": its elite at one with modern culture, its masses belonging to a more traditional world. In a provocative formulation, the Turks, he said, had rejected Mecca and were being rejected by Brussels (the European Union). Huntington foresaw trouble ahead. In a torn country, either the elites bring their people with them, or the popular culture rebels and reclaims political and cultural power. In this book, we have an essential and astute study of this fundamental, historic choice.

In a classic and admiring essay, "Atatürk as Founder of a State," written in 1968 by Dankwart Rustow, he left an enduring query and benchmark for Atatürk and his legacy: "Rousseau said of the founder of a commonwealth that he must be able to toil in one century and to reap in another. Ataturk's accomplishment in rebuilding the Turkish state in a national and modern image will be secure in proportion as the Turkish masses in the future will claim as their own his full inheritance." Rustow was writing in the 1960s, a mere three decades after Atatürk's death, when Atatürk's legacy seemed more secure and more accepted by Turkey's citizenry. Perhaps those appearances were deceptive, perhaps that deep culture of Turkish Islam lay dormant, waiting for a time of return and restoration. Some seven decades after his death, the hold of Atatürk on his country's political imagination has slipped, although in much of modern Turkey the founder would still recognize his work, his inheritance. But the Islamists are not his children; they don't dwell on the founder as they embark on their own journey and cast about in search of their own republic.

Although Baran does not take sides in this clash over Turkey's identity, she is, in a broad sense, a product of Turkish modernism. In these pages, you can see her concern for Turkish women and minorities and her refusal to fall for the false and easy temptations of anti-Americanism in Turkish politics. No one asks writers for solutions to great, enduring problems.

All we can ask is that they describe matters truthfully, fully and leave the judgment to others. Zeyno Baran has done this for Turkey; from her writing we can see the choices that Turks, and outsiders caught up in their politics, will be called on to make in the years to come.

Fouad Ajami
Senior Fellow, Hoover Institution
Cochairman, Herbert and Jane Dwight Working Group
on Islamism and the International Order

ACKNOWLEDGMENTS

I would like to thank Fouad Ajami, Charlie Hill, John Raisian, and the rest of the Hoover Institution team working on the Islamism and the International Order project for asking me to write this book. It is unusual for a project studying Islamism to explore Turkey, given the country's nine decades of secular democracy and six decades as NATO's only Muslim-majority member, which seemed to shield Turkey from the waves of Islamism that have swept other countries in the Middle East. Yet, as this book will, I hope, make clear, Islamism is also challenging Turkey's political and social order; whether and how Turkey will maintain its Western outlook and secular democratic system is far from clear and is the core focus of this book.

I had much help in putting this book together in a short time. Most importantly, my husband, Matthew Bryza, contributed tremendously, helping me think through my arguments and extensively editing each chapter. I could not have written this book without his energy. Onur Sazak, my research associate at Hudson Institute, made significant contributions as well, with his incisive support, insights and careful research into complex historical issues, especially the question of the nature of Turkish identity. Our intern, Aislinn Hettyey, provided invaluable assistance with a broad range of fact checks. I would also like to thank Megan Ring of Hoover Institution for her collaboration and cheerful attitude throughout this project.

I thank my colleagues at the Hudson Institute for their support throughout the time that I was writing this book. I am particularly grateful to CEO Ken Weinstein, who has provided crucial professional and personal support.

Introduction:
Turkey's Choice

Since the late 1940s, the United States and Turkey have enjoyed close military and political ties. The dawn of the Cold War nudged Turkey out of twenty-five years of isolation and into partnership with the Euro-Atlantic alliance. In the early 1950s, the country provided troops to the U.S.-led effort to blunt Communist expansion during the Korean War, and joined NATO as the alliance's southeastern bulwark against the Soviet Union.

For the next half century, Turkey viewed NATO as the cornerstone of its national security, while Washington and its NATO allies viewed her as a key partner in trans-Atlantic security. During the 1990s, this partnership deepened: Ankara supported Washington in the 1990–91 Persian Gulf War and allowed the United States to use İncirlik Air Base for politically sensitive missions; Turkey also contributed troops to U.S.-led operations in Kosovo and Afghanistan.

In the late 1990s, Ankara and Washington characterized their relationship as a *strategic* partnership; they worked together to ensure commercially reliable and environmentally safe transit of oil and natural gas from the Caspian Sea to global markets. The depth of American-Turkish cooperation was also reflected in the degree to which Turkey worked with Israel, the United States' closest and most controversial ally in the Middle East.

These five decades of close cooperation between Turkey and its NATO allies generated Western confidence that Turkey was a reliable ally and that its democratic system was sufficiently resilient to weather periodic political crises. American and European leaders generally accepted the victory of the Justice and Development Party (AKP) in Turkey's landmark 2002 parliamentary elections as another step in the nation's democratic evolution.

Some in the West worried about the AKP's roots in a politicized and socially restrictive strain of Islam that seeks to replace elected governments and secular law with Muslim regimes guided by religious law (*sharia*). But party leaders assured their Western counterparts that the organization's leaders had distanced themselves from Islamism to become "conservative democrats" (akin to Europe's Christian Democrats) and that an AKP government would sustain its predecessors' quest for European Union (EU) accession and economic reforms decreed by the International Monetary Fund (IMF).

In the wake of the September 11 terror attacks, the United States and its European allies were anxious for reassurance from the AKP. Western leaders acknowledged that the party had secured its victory in the 2002 election by relying not only on its conservative and Islamist base but also by attracting secular and liberal democrats. The leaders therefore initially hoped that Turkey had become the proverbial East-West bridge that could help contain the spread of Islamic extremism.

Given this history of fifty years of Turkey-NATO partnership and Western support for an AKP government, the plummeting popularity of the United States and Euro-Atlantic structures during the period of the AKP government is surprising—even shocking. According to the Pew Research Center, Turkish public approval ratings of the United States mid-2009 were at 14 percent—lower even than in Pakistan or in the Palestinian territories.[1] (Positive views of the United States among Turks had been as high as 52 percent in 2000, prior to the victory of the AKP.) Moreover, an earlier Pew poll (in June 2003) found that *82* percent expressed disappointment that Saddam Hussein's troops did not fight harder against the U.S.-led coalition.

Many analysts of Turkish affairs expected the public's approval of the United States to increase after President George W. Bush left office, given the broad disappointment and anger in Turkey over Bush's decision to launch the Iraq War. But even after a seemingly successful visit to Turkey by the newly elected Barack Obama, who chose that country as one of his first overseas destinations, support for the United States increased by only *two* points—from 12 percent at the end of Bush's term—which put Turkey *lowest* among all twenty-five countries surveyed in the 2009 Pew poll!

During the period of AKP rule, NATO's popularity has also suffered: Turks' support for the organization plummeted from 52 percent in 2005 to 35 percent two years later. Popular support for the EU also dropped sharply; in 2002, approximately 70 percent of Turks favored their country joining the EU, but by 2009, that number had dropped by more than half.[2]

While the approval ratings of the United States, NATO, and the EU were decreasing dramatically among Turks, the Iranian theocracy next door was becoming more popular. In 2002, 22 percent of Turks viewed Iran favorably; four years later, the figure had more than doubled.[3] That striking change stemmed in part from the stance of the AKP government: it has worked hard privately and publicly to improve cooperation with Tehran, coupling its embrace of Iran with sharp attacks on Israel—most notably, when Prime Minister Recep Tayyip Erdoğan verbally assaulted Israeli President Shimon Peres at the World Economic Forum in January 2009.

It is difficult for Americans and even many Turks to fathom the onset and persistence of such dismal ratings of the United States in Turkey. American visitors invariably speak of the genuine warmth they receive, while individual Turkish citizens have favorable views of President Obama and the Americans they meet. How can this seeming discrepancy be explained? Is the AKP stoking an anti-U.S sentiment (as when senior AKP leaders accused the United States of committing genocide in Falluja during the Iraq War)? Or are AKP policies and statements merely following public opinion? Is the anti-Westernism that has emerged during AKP governance a passing trend or a sign of a cultural and political transformation in Turkey, NATO's only Muslim member?

Even a tentative answer to those questions requires an understanding of the twentieth-century history of Turkey and, indeed, the Muslim Middle East. When Mustafa Kemal (later known as Atatürk), the father of modern Turkey and the Turkish Republic, built a new secular state in 1923 from the ashes of the Ottoman Empire, he set in motion a fundamental debate within Turkish society about the proper role of Islam in determining Turkish national identity. For Atatürk, a "Turk" was any citizen of the Turkish Republic, regardless of religion or ethnicity. Wanting Turkishness to be synonymous with modernity, he strove to modernize Turkey by establishing a government based on the rule of secular law, with Islam confined to the private sphere, and by pulling his country toward the West.

Atatürk's methods were severe, constituting a revolution from above. Virtually overnight, his reforms compelled former Ottoman subjects to alter their dress, social attitudes, and alphabet to conform to a new vision of a modern and secular Turkish Republic. Millions of people living in the Anatolian heartland resisted these changes. They continued to believe that being Turkish also meant embracing Islam as a key determinant of all aspects of life. In addition, many held onto folk traditions that had governed daily life in Anatolia for centuries.

These tensions in the Turkish identity between Islam's private and public roles, and between Turkey's Eastern traditions and its place in the West, have been playing out since the birth of the republic. The mass of Turks in Anatolia and poorer urban neighborhoods have gone through cycles of heightened religiosity, with Islam rising in prominence as a determinant of Turkish identity. Each time, those forces have been restrained by secular elites in Turkey's business community as well as its military and civilian bureaucracies who view themselves as the custodians of Atatürk's ideology (known as "Kemalism"). Samuel Huntington thus characterized Turkey in his seminal *The Clash of Civilizations and the Remaking of World Order* as a "torn country" between a secular elite and a conservative mainstream.[4]

Since the first years of the republic, the global Islamist movement has tried to tap into Turkey's conservative masses' resistance to Atatürk's separation of mosque and state. Beginning with the Muslim Brotherhood in Egypt in the late 1920s, Islamists have sought to expand Islam into a political ideology that (over time) could replace the rule of secular law in Turkey with *sharia*. Political Islam was strengthened by the 1973 boom in oil prices. The boom generated enormous revenues for Arab governments, which have helped finance Islamist efforts for the past four decades.

Turkey has been of particular importance to the Islamists, because the Ottoman Empire was Sunni Islam's last Islamic caliphate (or polity). Advocates of political Islam thus view restoration of the centrality of Islam to Turkish societal life as a crucial step toward resurrecting the caliphate and replacing secular governments around the world. While international Islamists understand that this utopian vision is unachievable in the near future, they are making great efforts to restore the role of Islam in modern society reintroducing *sharia* norms into public and private life and by pulling the world's Muslims together into a global community (or *umma*). The Islamists' most immediate strategic goal is to convince Muslims to define their identity primarily by their religion, and only secondarily as a citizen of their respective nations.

Key founders of the AKP spent three decades in Islamist organizations prior to Turkey's 2002 parliamentary election. Although they appear to embrace Turkey's democratic system, AKP leaders also seem to be implementing domestic policies aimed at restoring Islam's role in defining national identity and shaping society, while realigning Turkish foreign policy toward Islamist regimes (as in the Hamas-led Gaza, Sudan, and Iran).

Public opinion appears to be moving in the same direction as the AKP in both foreign and domestic affairs. According to an October 2007 Pew Research poll, among forty-two countries with a Muslim majority population, Turkey saw the second-largest drop in support for secularism during the five years since the AKP came to power: in 2002, 73 percent of Turkish respondents agreed that "religion is a matter of personal faith and should be kept separate from government policy;" by 2007, that figure had dropped to 55 percent.[5] A separate poll conducted in 2006 by the Turkish Economic and Social Studies Foundation (TESEV), a respected NGO, found that the number of people identifying themselves first as Muslims (as opposed to their ethnic identity or as Turkish citizens) grew from 36 percent in 1999 to 46 percent in 2006.[6]

That data, the AKP argues, indicates that it is not engineering a major reorientation, but merely following Turkish public opinion. The party seems convinced that most Turks increasingly favor the return of Islamic norms to Turkish society, while an elevated role for Turkey in its surrounding regions marks a return to diplomatic "normalcy."

But the struggle over the country's destination is far from settled. In the March 2009 municipal elections, the AKP won only 39 percent of the vote, rather than the 50 percent set by Prime Minister Erdoğan as a target. Polling data in January 2010 indicated that voter support for the AKP had dropped to around 30 percent. Growing numbers of non-partisan Turks have begun to wonder aloud whether Turkey is imperceptibly shifting toward Islamism, in the same way a frog fails to notice until too late that the water in which it is immersed is reaching the boiling point. Many recall their surprise in 1979 when they woke up to an Islamist revolution in neighboring Iran; and they were similarly shocked twenty-nine years later, when a young Turkish woman with an Islamic headscarf proclaimed on live TV: "I hate Atatürk; I admire Khomeini."

This book inquires into the fate of both Turkey's secularism and its democratic experiment. Growing numbers of Turks have wearied of the perennial tension between the Islamists and the secularists, and they favor neither *sharia* nor another military coup. For all the flaws of its political journey, the modern Turkish state has managed to maintain an essential separation between religion and the political realm. But that separation now lies in the balance. The Islamists who came to power via the ballot box have introduced great uncertainty into Turkey's political life: although they profess adherence to the basic principles of Turkish republicanism, they increasingly look like committed and skilled ideologues who have embarked on a major reorientation of the country's policies and practices at home and abroad.

CHAPTER ONE

Turkish Identity—from the Ottomans to Atatürk

The political tensions over what it means to be Turkish still resonate strongly between the AKP and its secular opponents. As previously noted, Atatürk defined a Turk as any citizen of the Turkish Republic, regardless of religion or ethnicity. He realized that the new state needed immediately to form a geographically based national identity, which could transcend the religious and ethnic divisions that had plagued the diverse groups inhabiting Anatolia and the Eastern Balkans. Otherwise, these regions risked being divided as a result of foreign military intervention following the collapse of the Ottoman Empire. But beneath the surface of this official definition of Turkishness, religious and ethnic factors continued to vie for a greater role in determining the national identity.

During the past few decades, Islam has been a more significant determinant of that identity. Religious nationalism, centered on the country's predominant branch of Islam, Sunnism, propelled the AKP to power. Historically, *religious* nationalism has generated hardship for Turkey's religious minorities (especially its largest group of non-Sunni Muslims, the Alevis, a heterodox Islamic sect that claims fifteen to twenty million adherents out of a total Turkish population of seventy-two million). Periods of *secular* nationalism have often generated hardship for the country's ethnic minorities, especially its largest ethnic sub-group, the Kurds. Today's secular nationalists are struggling to organize themselves into a viable political bloc that can oppose the AKP.

Comprehending the underlying dynamics of this current political struggle requires a deeper exploration of how the definition of Turkish identity has evolved over the course of the centuries.

Identity Vis-á-Vis the Ottoman Empire

The modern concept of Turkishness emerged in the Ottoman Empire in the mid-nineteenth century. Until then, the empire's ethnically diverse inhabitants thought of their nationality as Ottoman, though they often retained sub-identities as Turks, Greeks, Armenians, Jews, Bulgars, Albanians, et al. "Turk" was in fact a derogatory word; it defined Anatolian peasants who spoke Turkish and who adhered to customs rooted in the Turkic tribes that began migrating westward from the Altai Mountains (straddling present-day Russia and Mongolia) in the sixth century. The Ottoman sultans developed a concept of Ottoman nationality to bind their ethnically and religiously diverse subjects together. Not until the mid-eighteen hundreds, as nationalist doctrines gained momentum across Europe, did the concept of a Turkish identity began to take shape.

Identity was thus a complex concept during the Ottoman reign. Its evolution can be traced back to Sultan Mehmet II's conquest of Constantinople in 1453. The fall of the Byzantine Empire presented Mehmet II (or Mehmet the Conqueror) with the need to establish a new administrative system for his expanded empire. The system divided the empire's ethnically diverse subjects into political groupings based on their religious affiliation. Each religious community or nation was called a *millet*. Separate *millet*s were established for Muslims, Greek Orthodox Christians, Armenian Apostolic Christians, Syriac Orthodox Christians, and Jews. In this way, each group retained a sub-identity. All of the empire's Muslim populations, regardless of particular ethnicity within Islam, were grouped as the Muslim *millet*, and ruled themselves according to *sharia*. Officially, the Ottoman state considered the Turkic identity of the original Turkic tribes to be subsumed under the *umma*.

The fusing of political, religious, and ethnic determinants of identity was also evident in Sultan Selim I's decision—after defeating the Mamluks in Egypt in 1517—to establish Sunni Islam as the empire's state religion. The victory transferred the title of *Caliph* to the Ottoman Sultan from his Mamluk counterpart and transformed the Ottoman Empire into the *Caliphate*, the worldwide political authority for all Sunni Muslims.[1] Having acquired vast numbers of new subjects from diverse ethnic and religious backgrounds, Selim I needed a means to bolster the legitimacy of the ruling Ottoman family, and thereby hold his empire together. The new title of Caliph promised such legitimacy, at least among the large number of Arab Sunni Muslims, who now constituted the largest plurality among the *millets*. Moreover, designating Sunni Islam, the religion of the Ottoman family, as the *state* religion, differentiated the Ottoman Empire from its challenger to the east, Iran's Shia Safavid Empire. The Safavid rulers were also ethnically Turkic, and competed with the Ottomans for the loyalties of people living in the regions intersected by the two empires. Selim I was thus trying to define a primary "national" identity for his empire, determined by twin yardsticks: a political-legal factor (being the sultan's subject) and a religious factor (being a Sunni Muslim). In practice, establishing this new national identity proved difficult, given that the diverse populations within the empire persisted in adhering to their ethnic and religious sub-identities.

Officially, daily business in the Ottoman Empire was now conducted according to a version of *sharia* based on the Arabs' Sunnism. This interpretation of *sharia* consigned women, non-Sunnis, and non-Muslims to secondary status, though Christians and other non-Muslim *millets* were free to practice their own faiths, provided they paid taxes.

However, life in the Ottoman Empire did not change drastically with the adoption of Sunni Islam as the state religion. Even though *sharia* officially guided marital affairs, business transactions, and criminal matters, secular law was actually enforced at the personal discretion of the sultan, based on the Abbasid practice known as *kanun*, or administrative law. Although *kanun* was distinct from *sharia*, "The complex relationships between administrative law and *sharia*," as the Ottoman historian Norman Itzkowitz has observed, "would become a focal point of dispute in future reigns."[2]

Like their supreme rulers, who could also trace their ethnic roots to the Turkic tribes of Central Asia, Anatolian Turks did not simply abandon their traditions when Sunnism became the state religion of the Ottoman Empire. They instead maintained a sense of their own sub-identity based on the ethnocultural factor of the tribes' traditions, mixed with those the Anatolians acquired during their migrations.

Thus, Islam did not come to dominate all aspects of life for the Anatolian Turks. According to the earliest Turkic language inscriptions found in the Orkhon River Valley of present-day Mongolia, the original Turkic tribes were mostly pagans who adhered to shamanist practices. Even after they embraced Islam as they migrated westward, the tribes also adopted the humanistic traditions of tolerant faith and scientific learning that characterized Islamic thought in Central Asia (especially in Bukhara and Samarkand), in the tenth and eleventh centuries. This spirit of Bukhara and Samarkand confined religion to the private sphere, leaving science and civic affairs to be governed by rational thought. Such a mindset provided a natural foundation for the separation of mosque and state, and reflected the observation in the archaic Turkic text, *Kutadgu Bilig*, that the early Turkic tribes held governance and society above religion.[3]

The separation of the religious and secular realms blurred under the Seljuks, who emerged as the most powerful Turkic tribe in the ninth and tenth centuries. After defeating the Byzantines at Manzikert in 1071, the Seljuks established an empire centered in Anatolia and stretching to present-day Iran, Iraq, and Afghanistan. They had embraced Sunni Islam, which acquired powerful influence over their empire's government, politics, and culture. But in Anatolia, the Seljuks encountered a complex mix of secular traditions and religions, which preserved some degree of separation of everyday religious and civil life.

The above discussion demonstrates that both Seljuk and Ottoman policies aimed to merge political and ethnic differences into a single "national" identity based on Sunni Islam. But political and ethno-cultural factors persisted, preventing religion from becoming the pre-eminent determinant of national identity. That in turn facilitated the emergence of the Anatolian Turks' sub-identity. They were bound together by the ancient traditions of Central Asia and Anatolia and by the Turkish language. The latter differed from the language of the Ottoman court, where the palace elite spoke "Ottoman," a mix of Turkish, Farsi, and Arabic.

Geography played an important role in shaping the perennial battle between religious and non-religious factors, as well as national identities, in the empire. Both the Ottoman identity and the Anatolian Turkish sub-identity were rooted in the East, in the Turkic tribes' Central Asian and Anatolian ancestry as well as the traditions of Islam. Yet the Ottoman dynasty and its Anatolian subjects also sensed that their destinies lay toward the West, and they made numerous forays in that direction.

For centuries, Turkic tribes had been migrating westward. They had conquered Byzantium, a center of Western civilization in both the secular and spiritual realms. Mehmet the Conqueror had relied on a Hungarian cannon designer to manufacture the artillery that breached the previously impregnable walls of Constantinople. Under Süleyman the Lawgiver (known in the West as Süleyman the Magnificent), the Ottomans had extended their European conquests to Rhodes, Belgrade, and Budapest by the mid-sixteenth century, deepening their contacts with European ideas and technology. The Ottomans also expanded trade with the Europeans; Genoa and Venice maintained the trading colonies they had established under the Byzantine Empire, just across the Golden Horn from Constantinople. The Ottoman sultans brought European slaves to work in the Topkapi Palace as counselors and new troops (or *janissaries*) who served as the sultans' personal security force.

Though the Ottomans had anchored their empire in Europe to fulfill what they viewed as an inexorable Turkic-Islamic destiny to move westward, their attitudes toward the West remained ambivalent. They regarded Europeans as uncivilized—infidels, barbarians. The Ottomans detested travel to Europe, where they believed they could not learn anything new and would return home with diseases such as syphilis. The Ottomans acquired some new technology through trade. But pride in their imperial achievements deterred them from adapting their thinking to Europe's profound societal advancements during the Renaissance (and later the Enlightenment); they borrowed some European technologies but failed to adopt the new thinking that underlay them.

As a result, the Ottoman Empire began to lag behind Europe technologically, especially in the military sphere. In 1571, the Ottomans suffered their first naval defeat since the fourteenth century, when Holy League of Christian states routed their fleet at the Battle of Lepanto. That finished Ottoman domination of the Mediterranean, and for the first time, the Europeans gained confidence that the previously unstoppable force *could* be countered.

Despite their defeat at sea, the Ottomans continued their advance into Europe on land. In 1683, they reached the gates of Vienna for the second time in one hundred fifty-plus years. (The first was Süleyman the Lawgiver's unsuccessful siege in 1529.) In September 1683, following the Ottomans' two-month siege, Polish King Jan Sobieski led a combined Polish-Austrian-German-Tuscan-Cossack force that defeated the Ottoman-Crimean/Tatar-Romanian force besieging the city.[4] Though the war continued another sixteen years, the Battle of Vienna marked the end of Ottoman expansion into Europe and an iconic beginning of the empire's decline. The Treaty of Karlowitz, in 1699, memorialized the conclusion of the war and the acceleration of the Ottomans' decline.

That treaty, as Bernard Lewis points out, was a watershed event for the Ottomans.[5] Previously, they looked back on a millennium of westward expansion by Turkic tribes. Now, for the first time in the history of their empire, the Ottomans ceded sizable amounts of territory back to the Europeans: Hungarian lands returned to Austria, Podolia to Poland, and Dalmatia and the Morea (the Peloponnesus) were granted to Venice. The military and diplomatic defeat concluded by the Treaty of Karlowitz awakened many Ottomans to the reality that they lagged behind Europe and that their empire was in decay. In a century or so, such thoughts gave birth to a vigorous reform effort to absorb new ways of thinking from the West.[6]

For the moment, however, as the eminent Ottoman historian Niyazi Berkes argues, the Ottoman Empire was reduced from a major power *in* Europe to the status of a diplomatic pawn used *by* major European powers.[7] France, Austria, Britain, and Russia alternately allied with and opposed the Ottoman Empire as they managed their conflicts with each other. The Europeans also looked to the Ottoman Sultan and *Caliph*, the world leader of all Sunni Muslims, as the West's key interlocutor with Muslims to the East. It was during this period that the empire reinvented a new strategic role for itself as a bridge between East and West, supplanting its previous status as an Eastern power anchored to the West. Thus, Islam again grew in importance as a determinant of the empire's identity.

The Ottoman sultans of the early nineteenth century quickly checked the temptation to rely on Islam as their crutch for sustaining strategic relevance. As the doctrines of the French Revolution spread through their European holdings, the sultans recognized the vulnerability of their empire to exploitation by European powers and to disintegration under pressure from independence movements. To forestall those eventualities, Ottoman leaders realized they would need to attract Western technologies and modernize state institutions by secularizing them through Westernizing reforms. Mahmut II, who assumed the throne in 1808, emerged as one of the greatest reformers in Ottoman history. He eliminated the dangerously scheming *janissary* corps, which had repeatedly led religious uprisings against previous sultans, and developed a Western-trained standing army. Mahmut also sought to curtail the influence of the empire's leading Islamic authority, the *Şeyhülislam,* over the leadership of the Ottoman state. He began to secularize education by founding state schools specializing in technical and scientific studies, that functioned alongside the *madrassas* (Islamic schools) providing religious education.

Mahmut's reforms launched the Westernization of the Ottoman identity and–during the *Tanzimat* period, under his son and successor, Sultan Abdülmecit II—led to even more dramatic reforms. The new *Tanzimat* policies reflected an understanding that, as Greeks won their independence in 1832 and other nationalist movements gained momentum, existing religious, military, and civil institutions were no longer adequate to maintain the empire's territorial integrity. In an attempt to reintegrate these diverse nationalities into the empire, the Ottoman government provided greater rights to the sultan's non-Muslim subjects, who suffered second-class status under the *millet* system.

The *Tanzimat* period also produced a dramatic effort to secularize and modernize the empire's state institutions and thereby restrain Islam's societal role. That effort had a major impact on all aspects of life, leading to criminal and civil codes, a financial system based on that of France, the building of railroads and canals, the launching of the first universities and academies, and, in 1876, the codification of the first Ottoman constitution, which checked the authority of the sultan. The secular schools opened in the *Tanzimat* period were instrumental in the rise of free thinkers who, toward the end of the nineteenth century, led a new wave of modernization that would catalyze the re-emergence of a Turkish identity. The most famous graduate of these schools was Atatürk.

European diplomatic intervention undercut the ability of the *Tanzimat* reforms to stem the centrifugal forces of the empire's European minorities. At the end of the Crimean War, in the Charter of 1856, the Great Powers demanded and secured greater autonomy for ethnic communities than the Ottoman rulers had envisioned. The empire's Muslim population became convinced that Christian minorities enjoyed special privileges allowing them to prosper at the expense of the Muslims' economic well-being. That led to resentment culminating in a nationalist awakening of a Turkish identity and eventually to the "Young Turks" movement.

When Sultan Abdülhamit II assumed the Ottoman throne in 1876, movements for autonomy and independence were turning into tenacious insurrections in the Balkans. Abdülhamit's fear of imperial dissolution was severely heightened by Russia's declaration of war in April 1877 and victory over the Ottomans the following year. The Treaty of San Stefano, which ended that war, cost the Ottoman Empire its dominions in Europe, including those that later became the countries of Romania, Serbia, Montenegro, Bulgaria, as well as Armenia.

Abdülhamit II reversed the relative decline of Islam's societal role during the reigns of his two predecessors. He believed he could hold the crumbling state together and secure his authority by pushing a pan-Islamist ideology. By posing as a pious caliph and mediator among Britain, Russia, and the Muslim world, he passed as a respected leader—not only in the eyes of his Muslim constituents but also in the Western press. Despite the unraveling of the *Tanzimat* reforms in agriculture and economics, a meltdown of the Ottoman economy, and the suspension of constitutional rule and the parliamentary system, even the most rational and intelligent of Abdülhamit's subjects tended to be infatuated with his image as a powerful caliph, the "Shadow of God" on earth. He established strong ties with *shaykhs* (religious leaders), *ulema* (Islamic scholars), and other Muslim community leaders.

Returning to the fundamental ideas of Mehmet the Conqueror's *millet* system and Selim I's designation of Sunni Islam as the Ottoman state religion, Abdülhamit sought to unite all Muslims—regardless of their ethnic identity—under his caliphate. He brought the most powerful of Arab and Afghan *shaykhs* to Istanbul and gave them lucrative commissions to proselytize according to their strict interpretation of Islam, alien though it was to the empire's Turkic subjects. This period saw Ottoman identity particularly subsumed by its Muslim counterpart.

Not surprisingly, Abdülhamit's rejection of further Westernizing reforms accelerated both the decay of the Ottoman state and the independence of orthodox Christian nations, while his pan-Islamism failed to stem pan-Arabism. A reactionary pan-Turkic movement—the Young Turks—arose in response at the turn of the twentieth century. Although some of the movement's pioneers championed the Muslim component of the Turkish identity, the Young Turks' predominant idea was to create a new nation, known as *Turan*, based on the ethnic concept of unifying all Turkic communities from the Balkans to Central Asia. Language was a key factor in defining this nation. Over time, Turkish, as opposed to Ottoman, had become the language overwhelmingly used in Anatolia and eventually in parts of Thrace and the Balkans. The unifying power of the Turkish language deterred many Turks in Anatolia from joining the Arab nationalist and pan-Islamist movements taking hold at the time.[8]

As the Ottoman Empire collapsed in the wake of World War I, a true Turkish identity was emerging for the first time. Ethnicity now prevailed over Islam as the key element of this new Turkish nationalism. The Young Turks trumpeted their ethnic credo with the slogan "Turkey for Turks." The emerging military and political leader, Atatürk, born in 1881 in the culturally diverse city of Thessaloniki, bristled against this ethnic chauvinism. And drawing on the cosmopolitan education he received during the *Tanzimat* period, he proceeded to redefine what it meant to be Turkish.

Turkish Identity under Atatürk

This new and charismatic leader mistrusted the nineteenth-century nationalism based on ethnicity and religion, which he saw as having prompted the Balkan wars of liberation that led to the collapse of the Ottoman Empire. Atatürk understood that the Kurds in the East would be tempted to break away from the Ottoman territory to pursue their own sovereign state. At the same time, he worried that Abdülhamit's anti-Westernism and pan-Islamism were keeping the empire from the modernization required for survival.

Atatürk believed that Turkey's destiny was shaped by a constant pull toward the West. Ingrained with Western ideas from an early age, he received Prussian training as a soldier in the Ottoman army. His experience in both Western and Arab parts of the empire convinced him that Westernization was essential for Turkey to "take its rightful place among civilized nations." Atatürk concluded that, to modernize, Turkey would have to evolve from an Islamic state into a secular democracy, which protected individual rights through the rule of law.

Atatürk thus recognized the need for a national identity that could establish, unify, and preserve a new Turkish state. In 1920, the Ottoman monarchy accepted the humiliating Treaty of Sèvres with Greece, France, Italy, and Britain. The treaty preserved the Ottoman sultan's claims to the caliphate and Istanbul, but divided Ottoman lands among the Europeans, leaving only central Anatolia as "Turkey." Atatürk opposed the Ottoman government's readiness to partition the empire to save itself. He co-founded the National Movement to organize opposition to the government. In response to the Treaty of Sèvres, he convened the Turkish Grand National Assembly in Ankara as a new parliament and alternative political authority. And he took matters into his own hands by launching the Turkish War of Liberation.

Atatürk would engage Greek forces, which had invaded Anatolia with British support, and also confront the Italians and French, who had taken over parts of Anatolia. His defeat of those combined forces allowed Turkey to renegotiate the Treaty of Sèvres and avoid a Western land grab; the Treaty of Lausanne of 1923 established the borders of the Turkish Republic that remain today. Atatürk's victory also led the Turkish Grand National Assembly to abolish the Ottoman Sultanate in November 1922.

Atatürk sensed that in order to survive, this fledgling republic would need to unify its citizens through a new national identity. He advocated a Turkish identity embracing all ethnicities and religions found among the citizens of the republic. Thus, a geographically based political and legal factor— citizenship—supplanted religion as the primary determinant of Turkish identity. In stating that a Turk was a citizen of the Turkish Republic, rather than a member of the Muslim *millet* and the global *umma*, Atatürk was placing Muslims, Jews, and Christians on an equal footing, and thereby confining religion to the private sphere. In his mind, that would clear the way for his countrymen to adopt not just technology but also new ways of thinking from the West, which he believed were crucial to the Turkish Republic's survival and prosperity.

Atatürk, it should be pointed out, did not deny Islam's important role in determining the Turkish sense of self; nor did he deny the modern Turks' ethnic connection with their

Turkic ancestors. Instead, he tried to draw on the historical, cultural, geographical, and linguistic roots of the Turkish identity to create a Turkish or Anatolian Islam. By claiming that ancient Anatolian civilizations such as the Hittites and Sumerians were Turkish in essence, he tried to forge links between all the peoples of Anatolia.[9] Among Atatürk's greatest supporters were the Alevis, Anatolian Muslims who embraced a form of Shia Islam that incorporates elements of humanism and universalism and who had suffered under Sunni oppression for centuries. The leader's goal was to relegate Islam to the private domain as a source of moral and ethical behavior and teachings.

Atatürk established the Directorate of Religious Affairs (*Diyanet*) within the Turkish government to develop Turkish Islam and prevent the return of the Islamic mindset he believed had led the Ottoman Empire to disaster under Sultan Abdülhamit II. The *Diyanet* oversaw (and still oversees) all religious officials—as state employees—to prevent religious authorities from politicizing Islam. In an effort to connect Islam with Anatolia rather than Arabia, Atatürk changed the call to prayer to Turkish from Arabic. He abolished the caliphate in 1924 and eliminated Islam as the state religion of the Turkish Republic in 1937, a year before his death.

In keeping with his birth and educational grounding in the West, Atatürk recognized that to be strong and modern, Turkey must become a democracy. But democratic norms would come only with time, after the new Turkish state launched a dramatic reform program to establish a secular state, a modern society, and a Turkish identity in line with Atatürk's philosophy. After all, he was a military officer who did not believe in gradual and incremental changes; he pursued a top-down revolution of Turkish culture and institutions, capitalizing on the enormous political legitimacy he had earned as the savior of the nation. After replacing the sultanate with the Turkish Republic in 1923 and abolishing the caliphate the following year, Atatürk replaced *sharia* with the rule of secular law through the adoption of a civil code modeled on that of Switzerland. He banned *madrassas* and established a state system of secular schools focused on scientific learning to prepare students for modern life.[10]

Atatürk's approach to education reflected his conviction that "the most genuine guide in life is science." He changed Turkey's official language from Ottoman to modern Turkish and replaced the Arabic alphabet with its Latin counterpart; that tremendous modification quickly helped increase the literacy rate and moved people closer to the modern world, although it weakened their ties to their past. Turkey would now also adopt the Gregorian rather than the Islamic calendar.

Gender equality benefited significantly from the replacement of *sharia* with a civil code. Atatürk believed modernization required equal rights for women. He staunchly held that the oppression of women under *sharia* constituted a serious impediment to a nation's development. Atatürk asked, rhetorically, "How can a nation soar if half of the people are chained to the ground?"

Turkish women played an enormous role in the War of Independence; moreover, in traditional Turkic culture, they had enjoyed equal standing with men. In supplanting *sharia*, Turkey's new civil code banned polygamy and ensured women equal rights in divorce, inheritance, and child custody. Atatürk pushed for women to be educated, eligible for elected public office, and allowed to enter any profession. Turkish women gained the right to vote in 1930 and to hold elected office in 1934, sooner than in many Western countries. Atatürk forbade the Islamic headscarf for women (along with the fez for men) in favor of Western headgear, though the traditional Anatolian headscarf continued to be used, mostly by peasants.

Atatürk's reforms marked perhaps the most thoroughgoing restructuring of Turkish life since the Turkic tribes first departed the Altai Mountains. Implementing such a radical program required centralized authority with an efficient and powerful bureaucracy. To that end, Atatürk banned the Islamic Sufi orders. (He viewed the Sufi followers' strong allegiance to their *shaykhs* as a threat to the state's authority, and he regarded the Sufi orders' communitarian mentality as undermining individual liberty.) He founded and relied on the Republican People's Party to secure and execute political power in the Grand National Assembly.

As a soldier, Atatürk relied not just on civilians but on a military bureaucracy as well. In the preceding decades, the Turkish military had evolved into one of the country's most Westernized institutions, thanks in large part to its Prussian training. In subsequent decades, the military would gain the strong support of many Turks as a custodian of Kemalist ideology and the secular democracy Atatürk established.

Yet the military's later role in ousting four democratically elected governments underscores the peculiar nature of the democratic system Atatürk launched. A strong societal role for the military was perhaps inevitable in 1923, given the precarious circumstances under which the Turkish Republic was born. But nowadays the proper role of the military in the nation's political life is being debated as intensely as the proper role of Islam in society at large. In any case, Atatürk used his severe methods to lay the foundation for a modern state and a new Turkish identity based on separation of mosque and state, ethnic and religious tolerance, and respect for both religious and secular Turkic traditions.

Opponents of the monopoly of power Atatürk's ruling party enjoyed arose on the political left and right. Meanwhile, center-right politicians tapped into many conservative Turks' desire to restore Islam's former role in society. When Atatürk died in 1938, the foundation was laid for a resurgence of Islam in Turkish society, which played out in the Turkish Republic's first fully democratic elections in 1946 and, more decisively, in 1950.

CHAPTER TWO

The Rise of Political Islam and the AKP

Islam and Islamism in Turkish Politics from the 1950s to the 1980s

As has repeatedly happened throughout Turkish history, Islam made a comeback in Turkish society following Atatürk's passing, fueled by opposition to his authoritarian tactics, centralized political power, and embrace of Western values. A classic split was emerging between the political elites of the center (mainly in Ankara and Istanbul) and the conservative masses of the periphery (in Anatolia); this split would play out in the democratic decades that followed.

The Naqshibandi Sufis had significant influence over the Anatolian masses; they opposed Atatürk's decision to replace *sharia* with secular law and his emphasis on the political-legal supremacy of citizenship over Islamic religious affiliation in defining Turkish identity. Atatürk viewed the Naqshibandis' strict hierarchical organization as a threat to the authority of the state, with students surrendering their own thinking to their *shaykh's* spiritual, political, and social teachings. Atatürk also worried that the Sufis' emphasis on *umma* would undercut his Turkish identity based on citizenship. He therefore banned all Naqshibandi and other *tariqas,* or religious orders, that were based on a strict, top-down order.

The Naqshibandis nonetheless continued to operate underground. Their interpretation of Islam, which stressed *sharia*, sustained a social movement aimed at preserving the conservative Sunnism that Abdülhamit II had embraced. Parallel to their efforts, another movement had developed in the early twentieth century around Said Nursi, an Islamic thinker who wanted to merge Islam and politics even while appreciating the utility of Western science and technology. Nursi began his religious training in the 1880s with leading Naqshibandi *shaykhs*. In the first years of the Turkish Republic, he developed a large following. The Nurcus, or "followers of light" as they came to be called, opposed Atatürk's strong push for Westernization and strove to protect the cultural role of Islam. They grew into a powerful political force in the 1960s.[1]

Atatürk was nonetheless determined to press ahead with his historic reform agenda. Though a multi-party democracy was his ultimate goal, the Republican People's Party (CHP) ruled in an authoritarian manner and dominated Turkish politics until 1950. In that year, the Democrat Party, hewing to a more culturally conservative position, prevailed in the national elections, and its leader, Adnan Menderes, became Turkey's first democratically elected prime minister.

Menderes' party relied on the support of the masses of conservative voters on Turkey's political periphery. In contrast to the CHP's political base in the state's civilian and military bureaucracies, the Democrat Party still favored a central role for Islam in Turkish society. Menderes loosened the restrictive economic, political, and cultural policies, which Atatürk had put in place to channel the republic's development toward a secular democracy. Menderes' liberal economic policies favored free enterprise, but massive imports of foreign goods led to economic crisis and insolvency. He opened the door for a resurgence of cultural Islam. He reinstated Arabic as the official language of the call to prayer. He also established a faculty of divinity at the University of Ankara, as well as secondary schools for training prayer leaders (*imams*) and deliverers of sermons (*hatips*), known as the İmam Hatip Schools. Menderes' policies thus reintroduced religion into the public space.

Those policies agitated the secular establishment, which believed that Atatürk's vision of the Turkish Republic was being undermined. Though Menderes remained popular with voters on the periphery, he grew increasingly authoritarian in his second term, and was ousted by the Turkish military in a coup in May 1960. Tried and convicted of violating the Constitution, he was hanged in September 1961. Those who favored a greater role for Islam in Turkish society capitalized on that brutal act, rallying new followers with demands for a more "just" (i.e., Islamic) political system.

Severe economic and political instability plagued the 1960s. A serious economic recession late in that decade led to labor strikes, violent demonstrations, and political assassinations. Pro-Islam students and political groups united with right-wing nationalists to counter leftist student and worker movements; both sides carried out bombings, kidnappings, and assassinations. The Turkish political center had come apart.

Against the backdrop of political and economic chaos, efforts continued within Turkey to restore Islam's societal role. Such efforts were boosted by groups in the Middle East that had emerged earlier in the century with the aim of restoring Islam's place in politics and throughout their societies—in Turkey's case, after Atatürk abolished the caliphate in 1924. These groups aimed to promote not cultural Islam but *Islamism*, a political-religious ideology that maintains that a Muslim can practice "proper" Islam only in a state and society governed by *sharia*.

Islamists seek, over time, to establish a global community of Muslims (*umma*) who identify themselves *as* Muslims rather than as citizens of any country. The Turkish adherents developed an all-encompassing strategy to transform society into an Islamic state, embracing a top-down approach of securing political power as well as a bottom-up approach of shaping children's minds, beginning in elementary school.

The Muslim Brotherhood emerged as (and remains) the primary international group advancing Islamism. Formed in Egypt in 1928, its most influential thinker has been Sayyid Qutb, whose seminal work of 1964, *Milestones,* laid out both a grand strategy and tactical plan for Islamists to seize political power and replace secular governments with Islamist states by generating a critical mass of followers in government and society at large.

Beginning in the 1960s, Necmettin Erbakan emerged as a crucial conduit of the Muslim Brotherhood into Turkey. Erbakan was a former professor of engineering who had studied in both Turkey and Germany, winning election to parliament in 1969 as an independent from religiously conservative Konya.

In sharp contrast to the reformist spirit of the *Tanzimat* and Atatürk periods, Erbakan believed Turkey was in moral decay due to Western influences. He advocated purifying society by restoring Islam's predominant role in it. Erbakan was heavily inspired by the writings of Sayyid Qutb, particularly Qutb's call for the rural intelligentsia to organize itself and gradually gain control of the government from the urban elite. In 1970, with encouragement from a key *shaykh* of the Naqshibandi order, Mehmet Zahid Kotku, Erbakan formed Turkey's first Islamic political party, the National Order, to pursue these Islamist objectives. Erbakan became the political leader of the party, while Kotku provided its spiritual guidance. Kotku emerged as Turkey's most influential Naqshibandi leader and a link between some of the country's key leaders; in addition to Erbakan, Kotku's disciples included future President Turgut Özal and Prime Minister Recep Tayyip Erdoğan.

Throughout the 1960s, Erbakan's activism coincided with continuing societal chaos, as Islamists and far-right nationalists clashed with leftists and the economy floundered. In March 1971, the chief of the Turkish army's general staff handed center-right Prime Minister Süleyman Demirel a memorandum demanding the formation of a democratic government in line with Atatürk's reformist vision. This, the soldiers believed, would end the civil strife that was tearing Turkey apart.

Demirel's support was centered primarily among farmers and workers, rather than the secular elite. Eventually, he would emerge as one of Turkey's staunchest defenders of secular democracy while serving as President in the 1990s, and nowadays he enjoys wide respect as one of the "wise men" of the nation's politics. But in early 1971, Demirel balked at the general staff's directive to bolster democracy along Kemalist lines, and resigned. Martial law descended in April 1971 (and continued for two years). Turkey's military authorities shut down the National Order Party, and Erbakan went into exile in Germany.

A year later, Erbakan returned and established a successor to the National Order Party—the National Salvation Party. It was Islamism by another name. Erbakan's popularity grew. In 1974, he joined the coalition government of Prime Minister Bülent Ecevit, a social democrat whose lengthy political career included three terms as prime minister, the last one ending with the Justice and Development Party's landmark victory in November 2002. By partnering with Ecevit, Erbakan became Turkey's first co-leader of a national government to advocate the return of *sharia* and re-establishment of a religious state in Turkey. Erbakan, following Qutb's prescription, now helped members of the National Salvation Party and other Islamists gain positions of influence in institutions of the secular state.

Operating from his position of power, Erbakan expanded his Islamist efforts. They included rallying sentiment in Turkish communities abroad: in his 1975 manifesto, *Milli Görüş* (National Vision), he called on Turks living in Europe to identify themselves primarily as a community of Turkish Muslims and to avoid assimilation into mainstream European societies. The manifesto decried the de-Islamization of Turkey and called for a "just order" of society, meaning the return of Islam to a predominant position in determining national identity and organizing society; real justice, he argued, was impossible to achieve in a secular democracy. Erbakan's movement established chapters in Turkey and throughout Europe, propagating an anti-Western and anti-Semitic ideology that called— and still calls—for restoration of *sharia* rule in Turkey and relegates women to secondary status.

Meanwhile, violence and political chaos continued throughout the 1970s, with Islamists and leftists repeatedly clashing with right-leaning nationalists. In 1980, the Turkish military launched yet another coup. One result: the Constitutional Court banned Erbakan's National Salvation Party (and all other political parties). The party members were excluded from politics for "threatening national security and unity." Erbakan reemerged politically in 1983, launching yet another party, Refah (Welfare).

In 1980, the Turkish military reacted even more harshly against the leftists, because, in the midst of the Cold War, they were considered an especially grave threat to Turkey's secular democracy. In an attempt to reduce social tension and focus on the main political danger, the military tried to placate Islamists with a policy of "controlled Islam." Its goal was a "Turkish-Islamic synthesis," a new nationalism that em-

35

braced the predominant interpretation of Sunnism in Turkey and thereby aimed to shield pious Turks from international Islamist movements. To implement controlled Islam, the Turkish government restored mandatory (Sunni) religious education in secondary schools, broadcast religious TV programs, loosened controls on *tariqas*, increased the number of the Qur'an schools for young children, and greatly expanded the number of İmam Hatip schools (from 72 in 1970 to 382 in 1988).[2] Graduates of the religious schools, who had been permitted only to become clergy, were now allowed to enter all professions (except the military) and increasingly found positions in the government bureaucracy.

Turkey's secular leaders believed that by letting off some Islamist steam, they could prevent the societal pot from boiling over while they focused on what they viewed as the primary threats to democracy—leftist movements in general and communism in particular. This approach echoed that of the United States. In the wake of the Soviet invasion of Afghanistan in 1979, Washington viewed Soviet power and communist expansion as greater threats than the Islamism reflected in the Iranian Revolution that same year. As the cornerstone of its Afghanistan policy, therefore, the United States forged alliances with the Islamist *mujahedeen* against the Soviets and supported Pakistani President Zia ul-Haq's openings to Islamists in his country. Washington discounted the threat to democracy posed by the political Islam that swept Iran. Similarly, in Ankara, the technocratic government hoped it could maintain a controlled opening to Islam.

Ankara viewed the policy of controlled Islam as similar to Atatürk's attempt to create a Turkish Islam that reflected Anatolia's Islamic traditions rather than the Sunnism that had predominated in Arab lands for centuries. But whereas Atatürk and his successors in the Republican People's Party had implemented policies to keep Islam from regaining a predominant role in politics and society, the technocratic government removed many of those constraints. For example, in the 1930s, the government had established "village institutes" (*köy enstitüleri*) and "people's houses" (*halk evleri*) to channel rural Anatolians (especially women) toward secular attitudes. Village institutes provided vocational training that produced scores of teachers for secular schools, while people's houses focused on the arts and history in an attempt to produce Turkish citizens who embraced secularism and Western modernity along with the Islamic and secular traditions of Anatolia. During the political tumult of the 1950s, the Turkish government closed those institutions, fearing they were being used for communist indoctrination. Consequently, by 1980, the rulers lacked a key policy tool to calibrate the policy of controlled Islam.

The decisions of the Turkish military and the technocratic government following the 1980 coup thus cleared the way for Islamists to strengthen their political power and for Islam to regain momentum as a key determinant of Turkish nationalism. Fethullah Gülen was the leading Islamist thinker who took advantage of this opening. Gülen drew on and expanded the thinking of Islamist theorist Said Nursi, whose ideology sought to blend conservative Islamic social norms with science and technology from the West. Formerly a government-employed imam, Gülen established secular schools (as well as sporting and cultural organizations) across Turkey, the Caucasus, Central Asia, East Asia, Africa, and eventually even in the United States.

While these organizations carry on secular activities, Gülen's followers teach Islamic values and norms on the margins, especially in student dormitories. In the 1980s, Gülen's teachings about tolerance, peace, spirituality, science, and integration with the West became popular with Turkey's top secular leaders and were seen as the "real face" of Turkish Islam.

The leaders thus hoped that Gülen and his movement could nurture a national identity that would achieve Turkey's long-elusive goal: retaining Atatürk's focus on citizenship and Westernization while embracing an interpretation of Islam rooted in Turkish culture. In this same vein, the military looked to Turgut Özal, a World Bank economist in Washington during the 1980 coup, to restore stability by striking that balance in Turkish society. Over the next decade, Özal would emerge as one of the republic's most prominent leaders.

The military originally brought Özal back to Ankara as minister of economics to rejuvenate the economy through liberal reforms aimed at stimulating export-led growth and replacing the previous policy of import substitution. Özal's economic reforms succeeded, providing him with a political following. He formed the center-right Motherland Party, which triumphed in parliamentary elections in 1983. His tenure as prime minister lasted until November 1989, when he became president.

Özal was a disciple of Naqshibandi Sufi leader Kotku and previously a member of Erbakan's National Salvation Party. In the 1983 election campaign, Özal appealed to what he termed the long-repressed Muslim identity of Turks and promised a political leadership more sensitive to religious issues. During his rule, the number of Imam Hatip schools and mosques expanded. Özal also opened Turkey to Islamist finance—for example, banking according to *sharia* norms, which forbid interest. This led for the first time to a large influx of capital from Saudi Arabia, which follows the extremists' Wahhabi version of Islamism.

Özal's government repeatedly tried, but ultimately failed, to lift the ban on women wearing the Islamic headscarf in universities. During the 1980s, the headscarf became a political symbol for women who wanted to declare their adherence to Muslim beliefs as their primary identity. Previously, urban women generally did not wear a head covering, while rural women traditionally wore loosely fitting ones in the Turkish folk tradition. Following the Iranian Revolution of 1979, however, female university students in Turkey also began covering their heads with a scarf worn tightly around the face and neck to conceal skin and hair in the Islamist style. After the 1980 coup, Turkey's council of ministers and Constitutional Court banned headscarves for university students and public sector employees as threats to the secular principles of the republic.

Though Özal expanded openings for Islam in society under the policy of controlled Islam, it would be inaccurate to categorize Özal himself as an Islamist. Unlike Erbakan, he embraced Western ideas and even backed the United States (albeit belatedly) in the Persian Gulf War. His policies democ-ratized and liberalized Turkey, promoting an opening to the global economy and generating a new business elite (both sec-ular and Islamic), which strongly supported him.

Özal thus embodied the fusion of Islam and Westernization that was emerging as a modern Turkish identity. (His wife, leading a secular lifestyle and eschewing the Islamic headscarf, represented this fusion.) He enjoyed support from Islamists and liberals within Turkey, as well as from the West. Özal seemed to be the transformative figure Turkey's liberals had awaited to launch a so-called Second Republic. It would be based on Atatürk's achievements but would address the reli-gious concerns of conservative Muslims—as well as the com-plaints of the Kurdish and Alevi minorities who felt they had never obtained the rights and opportunities promised by Atatürk.

The Islamist Victory of the Mid-1990s— A New Vision for Turkey

When Özal died of an apparent heart attack in April 1993, Turkey lost its strongest economic manager and political leader on the center-right. His death ushered in a new period of economic and political instability. Ordinary citizens grew weary of constant political bickering between Turkey's center-right and center-left, and of the serious corruption that emerged during Özal's era and accelerated following his death.

This dissatisfaction worked to the advantage of Erbakan's Welfare Party, which in the 1994 local elections emerged as stronger than its counterparts in the major cities, finishing first in Istanbul and Ankara. The Welfare Party succeeded in winning over the center-left's traditional urban voters by promising to end corruption and to impose a "just order" rooted in Islamic traditions. While such pledges were not new in Turkish politics, urban voters viewed Welfare as more credible because the party's embrace of Islam made it seem morally "purer" than the discredited parties of the center-left and center-right. Moreover, Welfare's urban base grew as many rural voters, who had traditionally considered Islam a core element of their identity, migrated to the cities.

This burst in support for Erbakan's party set the stage for its landmark victory (with 21 percent of the vote) in the December 1995 parliamentary election. That marked the first time an Islamist political party had ever won a plurality in a Turkish national election. The result caused panic among the secular elite, prompting a political stalemate. The result: Özal's Motherland Party (now run by future Prime Minister Mesut Yılmaz) and Tansu Çiller's (also) center-right True Path Party formed a minority coalition government in March 1996. Three months later, the Welfare Party brought about the coalition's collapse through a censure vote in parliament. Rather than call for new elections, President Süleyman Demirel turned to Erbakan to form a new government. After Yılmaz refused to join with Erbakan, Çiller agreed to form a coalition and made Erbakan prime minister.

Turkey's first female prime minister (from June 1993 to March 1996), Çiller had earned a Ph.D. from the University of Connecticut and had acquired a small fortune through her husband's business ventures. She was thoroughly Western and an unlikely ally of the Islamist Erbakan. She even warned during the 1995 election campaign that her defeat and Erbakan's victory would bring Islamism to power. But she changed her mind during post-election negotiations with him over the formation of the new government, apparently hoping that Erbakan would moderate his Islamism once in power.

Çiller may also have been motivated by more personal considerations: once she agreed to form a coalition government with him, Erbakan dropped his threat to investigate corruption allegations against her. Contrary to Çiller's hopes, and those of many other members of the Turkish elites, Erbakan continued to challenge the secular establishment through Islamist policies. In 1994, he had advocated restoration of *sharia* to replace secular law, noting "of course it will be back; the only question is whether the process will be bloody or bloodless . . . we will make the process gradual so you will not feel any pain."[3]

As prime minister, Erbakan sought (but failed to achieve) gender-segregated buses and prohibition of alcohol in government-owned restaurants. He also pressed (and again failed) to significantly increase the number of İmam Hatip and Qur'an schools, as well as the lifting of the headscarf ban.[4] In foreign policy, he tried to reorient Turkey away from its pro-EU direction, and he created the "D-8" (Developing Eight nations) to promote economic and political unity among Muslim countries.[5]

Meanwhile, Fethullah Gülen's following continued to grow. His movement's cell-based, *tariqa*-style structure, together with a shift in his ideological emphasis, generated a cultlike devotion to Gülen. Before the mid-1990s, he had preached a spirit of tolerance that stressed the compatibility of Islam with secular democracy and the West. Now his agenda seemed to be moving beyond the cultural Islamic revival. Recordings of his lectures that surfaced in 1997 exposed the nature of his movement's closed meetings. They featured a crying Gülen who promised better days when the ideal Islamic society would finally be realized. Gülen advised his followers that "every method and path. . . . [including] lying" was acceptable to achieve a society whose foundation was Islam. He warned them to "keep our heads down until the situation is ripe. . . . until you have the power that is accumulated in constitutional institutions—in accord with the state structure in Turkey. . . ."

Many observers interpreted such language as an example of Islamic *taqiyya (dissimulation),* i.e., expressing public support for an accepted state policy to mask a hidden Islamist agenda. Fearing that such recorded statements indicated an attempt to infiltrate Turkey's police and military, and eventually overturn the secular regime, the Ankara State Security Court brought charges against Gülen. In 1998, he fled the country to avoid prosecution, and has since lived in the United States—from where he continues to direct a movement that has grown into the most powerful civil-society organization in Turkey.

Business, military, and civil-society leaders grew increasingly worried that the policies of Prime Minister Erbakan's coalition government and the separate activism of the Gülen movement were undermining Turkey's secular democratic system and Western orientation. The military issued public warnings suggesting a crackdown on such activities. Tensions peaked on February 28, 1997, when the military-dominated National Security Council (NSC) issued an ultimatum suggesting that the Welfare Party would be ousted from government and politics unless Erbakan ceased pursuing Islamist policies. As a result, he gave up his position in June 1997. Six months later, the Constitutional Court closed his party and once again banned Erbakan from active participation in politics.

Erbakan thereupon faded as a national political leader, but remained the leader of the Milli Görüş movement. He guided former members of his party, many of whom, in December 1998, founded the Virtue Party as a new Islamist expression. The Kemalists' counteractions against Erbakan's Islamist followers continued, and the pace of political party startings, stoppings, and shiftings accelerated: in June 2001, the Constitutional Court closed down the Virtue Party; Erbakan and his followers then founded the Felicity Party (which still exists but with a small following); in August 2001, a reformist Milli Görüş faction formed the Justice and Development Party (AKP).

The AKP's Rise and Victory

The key founders of the AKP, former Istanbul Mayor Recep Tayyip Erdoğan, former Welfare Party spokesman and minister Abdullah Gül, and former parliamentarian Bülent Arınç, had all shaped their political identities and careers within Erbakan's Milli Görüş movement and his political parties. The AKP was more a broad movement than a unified party. Erdoğan, Gül, and Arınç each represented separate currents within Erbakan's wing. Erdoğan had the support of the Naqshibandis as well as connections to international movements like the Muslim Brotherhood; Gül represented the moderate wing of the Welfare Party, which sought coexistence with Turkey's secular authorities; Arınç had deep connections with the Gülen movement, and represented more aggressively anti-Kemalist elements among Erbakan's followers.

Erdoğan (born in 1954) was perhaps the most prominent of these three future leaders of the AKP. Elected mayor of Istanbul in 1994 on a Welfare ticket, he catapulted into the national spotlight as the head of Turkey's commercial and cultural center, a city of 11 million inhabitants. His charisma and Islamist messages attracted the concern of Kemalist authorities in Ankara. While mayor, Erdoğan famously said, "Democracy is like a streetcar. You ride it until you arrive at your destination, and then you step off," and "We believe that democracy can never be the objective; it's only a tool." Supporting the return of *sharia*, he also said, "The statement that sovereignty unconditionally belongs to the people is a huge lie. Sovereignty unconditionally belongs to Allah." Erdoğan further declared, "Praise to God; we are all for *sharia,*" and "One cannot be secular and a Muslim at the same time. You will either be a Muslim or a secularist."

Erdoğan made his most significant statement in December 1997, at a rally in the southeastern town of Siirt, where he quoted the following passage from a poem: "The mosques are our barracks, the domes are our helmets, the minarets are our bayonets, and the faithful are our soldiers." That got Erdoğan convicted of subversion for "praising fundamentalism and violating a law that bans 'provoking enmity and hatred among the people.'"[6] The conviction followed the Welfare Party's ban earlier in 1998. In 1999, Erdoğan began serving a ten-month term in jail; freed after four, he remained banned from politics.

Erdoğan's imprisonment and banning shocked the new generation of Islamist leaders. As they looked to the future, they recognized the need for a more patient approach and a political movement that would build support for a greater political role for Islam within the structure of Turkey's secular democracy. The AKP's founders thus decided to break with Erbakan's confrontational approach. They set out to build a center-right political party that could attract both pragmatic Islamists who were willing to work within the democratic system and liberal democrats who sought greater social, political, and economic freedoms. They were inspired by the outlook and political approach of Turgut Özal, whose Motherland Party united the business community, liberal democrats, the previously mentioned "second republicans," and *tariqas* into a big, diffuse party.

To broaden their appeal beyond conservative Islamic voters, AKP leaders reframed their language, restraining Islamist slogans and stressing democracy, rule of law, and justice as universal values. They incorporated Turkey's EU accession into their platform and pledged to continue Turkey's cooperation with the IMF, marking additional breaks with the Islamist parties of the past. The AKP also stressed the centrality of NATO and partnership with the United States and Israel to Turkey's national security. In short, the AKP was trying to define itself as a conservative democratic party, akin to Europe's Christian Democrats.

As the party's leaders looked ahead to parliamentary elections scheduled for November 2002, they carried the above messages to voters through personal engagement with secular business leaders, intense media efforts, and grassroots outreach to the poor. To Turkey's elite business leaders, many of whom had centered their commercial empires in media holding companies and banking, the AKP made the case that they sought to expand Turkey's economy (as Özal had done) and strengthen democracy. AKP leaders claimed that they had evolved from the Islamism of Erbakan's Milli Görüş and his Welfare Party, and now posed no threat to the lifestyles of Turkey's business elite.

At the same time, the party began creating its own media outlets, drawing initially on the Gülen movement's newspapers and television network. As the Welfare Party had done in the previous elections, the AKP also reached out to poor voters, whom existing secular parties had largely ignored, promised to clean up the corruption that characterized the political elite, and offered financial assistance—even free food and coal—to needy families. Again, following the footsteps of the Welfare Party, the AKP cultivated Turkey's largest ethnic minority, the Kurds, and even some of the Alevis, by promising new openings in democratic and cultural rights.

Meanwhile, the secular political parties were losing support. Their credibility had suffered a severe blow back in 1996, before the formation of the AKP, when a senior national police official, a drug smuggler/murder suspect, and a pro-government vigilante were found in an automobile that crashed near the town of Susurluk in western Turkey. The investigation of this "Susurluk incident" uncovered an alleged conspiracy among the car crash victims, under government orders, to plot political assassinations. The probe expanded into alleged links between government security agencies, right-wing death squads, and criminal gangs that extended back to the early 1990s, dealing a serious blow to the established secular parties.

Throughout the '90s, the secular political leaders continued their bickering and fomented political instability against the backdrop of economic difficulty that had characterized Turkish politics for decades. Turkey endured ten coalition governments between 1991 and 2002, with each lasting at most two years. Allegations of massive corruption forced Mesut Yılmaz to resign as prime minister in 1998. The coalition governments proved dysfunctional and incapable of managing the growing economic problems. These economic tensions grew into a full-blown financial crisis in February 2001, when President Ahmet Necdet Sezer threw a copy of the Turkish constitution at Prime Minister Bülent Ecevit at a cabinet meeting, accusing the government of failing to advance reforms and combat corruption in the banking system.

Such political theatrics had a devastating financial impact. The value of the Turkish lira plunged by nearly 50 percent, consumer prices skyrocketed, and hundreds of thousands lost their jobs. Inflation almost doubled from 39 percent the previous year to 68 percent in 2001. Economic growth dropped from 6 percent the previous year to -7.4 percent. The corrupt banking system, which had led to the ousting of Prime Minister Yılmaz, collapsed. Turkey's financial system and economy were in freefall, and its political leaders were unable to resolve the crisis.

In spring, the IMF stepped in, with strong U.S. support, to help avert an economic catastrophe. The IMF offered a $12-billion loan program, on top of its existing $10-billion loan, which would make Turkey's overall program the largest in the IMF's portfolio. To secure these funds, Turkey would have to design and implement a sweeping reform of its banking system and entire economy. Conceding that his government was unable to develop such a reform program, Prime Minister Ecevit called for outside help, tapping a Turkish economist and vice president of the World Bank, Kemal Derviş. He made dramatic reforms, and they worked: by late 2001, the Turkish nation's financial system and economy were beginning to recover.

Derviş was hailed as the savior of the economy. He grew enormously popular among secularists, who viewed him as a potential national leader and counterweight to the Islamist alternative of the AKP. In the summer of 2002, Derviş tried to form a new liberal party with a full-blown commitment to a secularist agenda. His effort ultimately failed, leaving the center-right and center-left without alternatives to the leaders who had discredited themselves through years of corruption, economic mismanagement, and a near-fatal financial malaise.

Turkey's 2001 financial crisis spawned a popular yearning for an entirely new generation of political leaders. This "throw-the-bums-out" mentality won the AKP additional support, even among many secular voters, who believed the party would sustain the Derviş reforms, curtail corruption, and thus restore economic stability. While some among the secular supporters of the AKP were concerned about a possible Islamist "hidden agenda," they were willing to give the party a chance. They reasoned that the democratic process itself—or the military if need be—would rein in leaders who tried to institute unacceptable policies.

It was clearly the AKP's moment. The party was even able to capitalize on its nickname, "AK," which means "white" or "clean" in Turkish. The new voters it had attracted complemented a solid base throughout Anatolia of conservative voters, especially emerging Islamic business leaders, who had felt slighted for decades by the secular magnates of the economic mainstream.

On November 3, 2002, the AKP won a dramatic victory in parliamentary elections. Its 34.3 percent of the vote translated into a majority of the seats in parliament, given that only one other party crossed the 10 percent threshold. The AKP was thus able to form the first single-party government in Turkey since 1987, giving millions of Turks across the political spectrum hope for a return to political and economic stability.

The AKP owed Erbakan a deep debt of gratitude for its electoral victory. During the course of three decades, he had laid the ideological and operational foundation for the party's eventual political success. Throughout that period, Erbakan had been relentless. When one party he headed was banned, he returned with another one bearing a different name. It could be said of him that he saw the promised land of an Islamist Turkey, but was not fated to enter it.

A younger generation of Islamists would pick up his torch. They learned from his errors and stepped forth to claim political power in their own right. They were keen to let the political process play out, proclaiming enough fidelity to the guiding principles of the Turkish republic, as they kept their gaze fixed on their own political model: a workable alternative to the secularism of the preceding eight decades.

CHAPTER THREE

The AKP's Political Victories

Frustrating Hope for Democratic and Europeanizing Reforms

As the AKP prepared to capitalize on its landslide victory in the 2002 parliamentary election, it proceeded with care. The party's leadership remained in a complicated position with its chairman, Recep Tayyip Erdoğan, still banned from politics. Initially, the government was headed by Abdullah Gül as prime minister. During its first few months in power, the party's parliamentary majority voted to nullify the political ban against Erdoğan. In March 2003, he won a seat in a by-election in Siirt (his wife's hometown and, ironically, the city where he read aloud from the poem that led to his imprisonment). He then became prime minister, with Gül shifting to foreign minister.

A cautious spirit continued to guide the AKP at the outset of the Erdoğan government. The party sought to consolidate its support domestically and abroad by cultivating an image of a conservative (e.g., religious) and democratic party, akin to Europe's various Christian democratic parties. Gül and Erdoğan focused their public statements on economic reform and growth, and Turkey's quest for EU membership. The Turkish government sustained the economic policies outlined by Kemal Derviş's reform plan and sanctioned by the IMF.

Those policies of continuity reassured domestic and international audiences. At home, growth returned to the Istanbul stock market and the Turkish economy, which deepened the business elite's support for the AKP. Abroad, the government won accolades from U.S. and European leaders as a new and hopeful type of political movement that could prove the compatibility of Islam and democracy and blunt the appeal of extremists following the terrorist attacks of September 11, 2001 and March 11, 2004. American and European officials cheered the Erdoğan administration's success in securing parliamentary approval of its first constitutional reform package in July 2003. In accordance with EU norms, these reforms *inter alia* curbed the role of the military in Turkish politics by mandating a civilian head of the nation's most powerful state security body, the NSC, and diminishing its policy-making authority; the latter step was deemed necessary because the military continued to wield heavy influence on the council even without chairing it. AKP leaders hailed these reforms as proof of their commitment to rejuvenate and strengthen Turkey's democracy.

In December 2004, a favorably impressed European Council voted to invite Turkey to begin accession negotiations for

EU membership, capping a 40-year quest by successive Turk-ish governments to be granted EU candidacy. Accession talks commenced in October 2005.

But the AKP leadership also began to send contradictory signals. Rather than stressing their commitment to democ-racy, key leaders suggested that the Islamist agendas of Erba-kan and the Gülen movement remained active. In 2003, Ömer Dinçer, a key AKP strategist and an undersecretary at the prime ministry, announced his continued embrace of the Islamist ideology and tactics that he had outlined in a famous speech in 1995, when he was a member of Erbakan's Welfare Party.[1] In that speech, Dinçer welcomed what he termed the uniting of cultural Islamic movements, such as that sparked by Gülen, with Islamist political parties to replace the current republic with an Islamic state governed by *sharia*.

Echoing Dinçer's attitude, the AKP government seemed to adjust the direction of EU-mandated reforms away from deeper democratization and toward the reintroduction of Islam into public life. In 2004, Prime Minister Erdoğan cited the EU requirement of reforming Turkey's penal code to jus-tify his own call for the criminalization of adultery. This move disturbed many because it would mean the reintroduction of *sharia* norms into private family matters, a step that would weaken the secular legal order. In a similar move, the govern-ment invoked the EU's call to expand religious freedom—a step that many secular Turks perceived as an attempt to lay the foundation to overturn Turkey's legal ban on the Islamic headscarf in universities. Both of these social reforms ultimately failed in the face of sharp criticism from the Kemalist opposition, women's groups, newspaper editorialists, and other civil-society groups.

A few European officials echoed growing concern within Turkey about the AKP's apparent attempts to divert reforms in the name of EU accession from democratization to private social matters. As the EU debated the acceptability of public displays of religiosity within Europe's secular democracies, members of the European Court of Human Rights (ECHR) broke with the European mainstream and expressed greater understanding of Turkey's restrictions on wearing the headscarf. In November 2005, the ECHR upheld Istanbul University's 1998 decision to forbid it there. The court judged the ban legitimate in the Turkish context because of the effect that "wearing such a symbol, which was presented or perceived as a compulsory religious duty, may have on those who chose not to wear it." The court noted the importance of protecting secularism and equality, two principles that "reinforce and complement each other," as well as the Turkish constitution's emphasis on safeguarding the rights of women.

The ECHR's ruling shocked the AKP and dampened enthusiasm for membership in the European Union. Prime Minister Erdoğan declared, "This court cannot reach such a decision. They should ask religious people, the *ulema* [Muslim theologians]."[2] In the months following the ruling, AKP leaders stepped up efforts to soften the constitution's strict protections of secularism. On April 23, 2006, the anniversary of the founding of the secular parliament, Speaker Bülent Arınç told his legislative colleagues that the constitutional principle of secularism should be redefined to maintain separation of mosque and state without stifling public expressions of private piety. He added that the practice of "intense secularism" should not turn society into a "prison."[3] Arınç's speech was interpreted as a call for constitutional reforms to lift the head-scarf ban and clear the way for the general return of Islamic norms to mainstream society.

Meanwhile, the AKP was shoring up its power throughout society. It placed its followers in positions in all the civilian bureaucracies, including the courts. Many of these appointees were the party's most conservative advocates for the return of Islam into public life (for example, the graduates of İmam Hatip schools—see Chapter 4). The AKP also supported the growth of the Islamic business elite. State contracts were channeled to its supporters, many of whom belonged to the Naqshibandi orders and the Gülen network. Small and medium businesses that began moving from the Anatolian periphery to urban centers under Özal had given birth to a new elite in Istanbul.

The AKP's first four years in power achieved mixed results. On the one hand, the initial package of constitutional reforms boosted Turkey's democracy and EU aspirations, while its economic policies sustained stability and growth. Such policies gained the AKP many non-Islamist supporters, including members of the secular business elite. But by continuing their predecessors' practice of using political power to provide economic benefits to themselves and their allies, AKP leaders frustrated the hopes of millions of centrist voters who longed for more democracy, less corruption, and justice and development for all. Moreover, as the AKP consolidated its strength, staunch Kemalists worried that they had lost power for the foreseeable future, and that Islam was regaining its societal role.

The Kemalists Counterattack

As expected, the Kemalist elite strongly opposed the AKP's initiatives on Islamist reform and political consolidation. A central figure in the resulting counterattack was the president of the republic, Ahmet Necdet Sezer. A former chairman of the Constitutional Court, Sezer was a staunch believer in Turkey's secular democratic order. The holder of that office had traditionally been viewed more as an apolitical arbiter than as the executive of government policy, and thus as a key element in Turkey's system of checks and balances. The president's core functions, besides serving as head of state, are to approve or veto all parliamentary bills and all senior appointments of state officials, including generals, governors, and university rectors.

In Sezer's hands, the presidency was the Kemalists' last remaining lever to restrain what they viewed as a serious erosion of the secular order. Sezer carried out his duties with vigor. He vetoed Prime Minister Erdoğan's candidate for the central bank presidency, Adnan Büyükdeniz, who headed a financial institution practicing *sharia*-based banking methods. He blocked university-rector nominees whom he feared would not enforce the headscarf ban. In addition, he vetoed several key AKP bills: in 2004, a bill that proposed fundamental changes to the Higher Education Law in order to facilitate İmam Hatip graduates' access to higher education institutions; in 2007, a constitutional reform package that included amendments to elect the president by popular rather than parliamentary vote.

In his public speeches, President Sezer increasingly warned against "creeping Islamization" of the Turkish republic. In his opening address to the Grand National Assembly in October 2006, Sezer warned of an Islamist threat by the AKP. He repeated his warnings in April 2007, during an address to the officer corps at the War Academy. He told the audience there that domestic and foreign entities were trying to Islamize Turkey under the false pretense of democratization.

That second warning was strategically placed: President Sezer's key ally in countering the AKP's pro-Islam policies was the military. In the past, the Turkish general staff had intervened at key political moments to "preserve secular state order" through decisions of the NSC and, more dramatically, through coups. Despite its sometimes heavy-handed tactics, the military had never intervened against governments that enjoyed strong public support, and as a result, had for decades remained Turkey's most popular government institution. Turks generally accepted its self-appointed role as protector of the model of secular democracy, though many Islamists and adherents of the political left retained deep distrust of the military as an enemy of democratic freedom. Despite the 2003 reforms that reduced the general staff's political influence, the military retained significant authority and had no qualms about exercising it.

While General Hilmi Özkök, as chief of the general staff from 2002 to 2006, sought political stability through accommodations with the AKP, his successor, General Yaşar Büyükanıt, was more outspoken in opposing what he viewed as the AKP's efforts to weaken secularism. Opening the academic year at the Military Academy in October 2006, General Büyükanıt warned that Turkey's secular democracy was threatened by "Islamist fundamentalism" and asked rhetorically, "Are there not people in Turkey saying that secularism should be redefined? Aren't those people occupying the highest seats of the state? Isn't the ideology of Atatürk under attack?" The following year, at the Turkish Embassy in Washington, D.C., Büyükanıt warned that the republic had not faced graver dangers since 1919, before the start of the War of Liberation, and made clear that the military would not allow the country to disintegrate.

Election Showdown: The AKP Blinks

The 2007 political season promised to be monumentally important, as Turkey looked ahead to parliamentary election of a new president in April and a new parliament in November. The AKP was confident that it could attract enough independent legislators to secure the two-thirds majority required to propel its candidate to victory, regardless of opposition from the only other party represented in parliament, the Kemalist Republican People's Party (CHP).

Erdoğan seemed to ponder for months whether he would *be* the AKP candidate. His critics said he was not suitable, arguing that he would politicize the office, had spent time in jail for opposing secularism, and had a wife who wore an Islamic headscarf, which was seen as a political statement. Media speculation swirled around whether Erdoğan would risk a direct confrontation with the Kemalist elite as the AKP candidate or disappoint the AKP's Islamist base (and risk splitting the party) by giving way to a candidate with no Islamist background, such as Defense Minister Vecdi Gönül (whose wife did *not* wear a headscarf). In the end, he and the party leadership settled on Foreign Minister Abdullah Gül. As a co-founder of the AKP with a long history in Erbakan's parties and a wife who wears the scarf, Gül was acceptable to the party base. The AKP leadership hoped that Gül's moderate rhetoric and conciliatory demeanor would help temper Kemalist opposition.

The Kemalists, however, were not placated by the relatively moderate stance of candidate Gül, especially given Speaker Arınç's statement that Turkey's next president should be "religious."[4] The CHP counterattacked in parliament, arguing that the AKP's near-two-thirds majority did not reflect an overwhelming mandate, since it resulted from a mathematical anomaly rooted in the peculiarities of the country's election laws. It called for the election of a *new* parliament, which theoretically would more accurately reflect the electorate's current preference, before parliament elected Turkey's next president. But Erdoğan and the AKP refused to hold the parliamentary election earlier than planned, which meant the presidential election would occur first.

As parliament convened for the first round of presidential balloting on April 27, the CHP leaders attempted to block the vote on procedural grounds. They claimed that the constitution required a quorum of two-thirds (or 367 deputies, four more than AKP's number of seats) to validate a presidential vote, even though that alleged requirement had never been invoked in previous presidential elections. All CHP deputies and several independents staged a boycott, cutting attendance to 361. The AKP majority nonetheless proceeded with the vote, electing Gül as president. The Kemalists responded by lodging a protest case with the Constitutional Court declaring the presidential vote illegitimate due to the lack of a quorum.

Late that same evening, the Turkish military stepped into the fray, posting a sharp warning on the website of the general staff. The statement cautioned that the military considered itself an "absolute defender of secularism" and underlined an April 12 press statement by General Büyükanıt that Turkey's next president must be "committed to the principles of the Republic not just in words, but in essence, and demonstrate this [commitment] in actions."

On May 1, the Constitutional Court ruled that a quorum of 367 MPs was indeed required to validate a presidential election. On May 10, Gül withdrew his candidacy. The next day, parliament voted to move up the parliamentary election nearly three months, to July 22. The Kemalists appeared to have prevailed, having blocked Gül's election and set a precedent of requiring a quorum they could use in the future to prevent the AKP's choice of a presidential candidate. The outraged Erdoğan called the court's decision "a shot fired at democracy." Many others thought that the general staff's online manifesto had clouded the court's independence, and (referring to the online posting of the warning) spoke of an "e-coup."

Secularists *vs.* Islamists: "No *Sharia*, No Coup"

The high political drama and constitutional crisis of spring 2007 reflected a key political fault line in Turkish society. On one side of the divide were the AKP's heterogeneous supporters, split into two schools. On the right of that divide: devout Muslims and Islamists, who formed the AKP's base and expected the party to deliver on their core demands—above all, a constitutional amendment to permit women to wear the Islamic headscarf in universities and government offices. On the left of the divide: the so-called liberal democrats, who welcomed the AKP's political and economic reforms, hoped the party would improve the plight of Turkey's Kurdish population, and shared the AKP's sharp opposition to the military's accustomed role in politics. (The military had repressed many of the liberal democrats following previous coups.)

Opposing the AKP camp was a similarly loose alliance of traditional secularists and nationalists who demanded preservation of the republic as a unitary, secular, and democratic state. They feared that the AKP would expand Islam's role in the public sphere and grant autonomy to the Kurds, all at the expense of Turkey's secular democratic institutions and perhaps its territorial integrity. Although previously pro-Western, the secular camp perceived the United States and Europe as supporting the AKP and its politico-religious aspirations, given their continuous praise of the AKP and its policies. Some extreme secularists asked why the military was "tolerating" the AKP instead of treating the party the same way it had treated Erbakan less than a decade earlier.

As the electoral-constitutional crisis flared in April, the divide between these two camps played itself out on the streets through mass demonstrations. Following small rallies by AKP supporters in İzmir and Balikesır, the proponents of secularism launched large ones. On April 14, close to one and a half million protestors took to the streets of Ankara, chanting their support for Turkey's secular and democratic principles and urging Erdoğan not to run for president. They waved Turkish flags and chanted slogans such as "Turkey is secular and will remain secular!" and "We don't want a *sharia* state!"

A similar rally took place in Istanbul on April 29, two days after the military's anti-Islamist electronic statement. The secularists continued their mass protests even when Gül withdrew his candidacy for president on May 10, shifting their focus to parliamentary elections. Large gatherings took place on May 13 in the Aegean city of İzmir and a week later in the Black Sea port of Samsun (two critical cities in Turkey's War of Liberation in 1920).

The secularists who had taken to the streets were an eclectic mix of largely moderate people. Many had never taken part in a public demonstration. More than half were women who feared that an Islamist president would undermine their status as equal citizens. Their pleas for the defense of Turkey's secular and democratic order were at times overshadowed by a small, radical group calling for military intervention to prevent the election of an Islamist president.

The large majority of protestors were uncomfortable with both the AKP's push to soften Islam's separation from public life and the extreme secularists' push for the military to remove the AKP from power. Their most prevalent slogan during the rallies was "No *sharia,* no coup!" That was the middle road—the demand for a political process that would normalize political life by maintaining the separation between religion and politics, while keeping the military in its barracks.

The AKP Rebounds with Electoral Wins

The large demonstrations of April-May 2007 set the tone for the final weeks of campaigning for the July 22 parliamentary election. The pro-secular camps urged both the center-left and center-right parties to form separate electoral blocs that could surpass the 10 percent threshold to avoid a repeat of the disproportionate majority the AKP won in November 2002. Neither centrist bloc materialized, however, and Turkey's center-right parties melted away. Meanwhile, the AKP ran a successful campaign portraying itself as a centrist party seeking democratic reform and economic growth. The AKP's economic record was indeed strong: annual GDP growth during the party's first years in office averaged 7.4 percent, compared with only 3.7 percent during 1991–2001; inflation had fallen by 2004 to single digits for the first time since 1976, after soaring to 68 percent in 2001. AKP supporters argued that the party had been unfairly victimized by the Kemalists' attacks.

On election day, the AKP camp succeeded in rallying even more voters from the center of Turkish politics than it had attracted in November 2002. Many business leaders previously associated with the secular camp voted for the AKP in the expectation of continued economic stability. The party won a resounding victory, expanding its share of the vote to nearly 47 percent (from 34 percent in 2002) and exceeding projections in national polls during the early summer of 2007. At the same time, a third party, the rightist Nationalist Action Party (MHP), joined the AKP and the CHP in breaching the 10-percent threshold for parliamentary representation. That development meant that AKP's 2007 victory translated into fewer parliamentary seats (341) than in 2002 (363 out of 550, or four shy of a two-thirds majority).

The AKP's room for maneuver narrowed as 22 candidates of the Kurdish Democratic Society Party won parliamentary seats. This allowed the Kurdish party to organize itself as an unofficial bloc, even though it won less than 5 percent of the national vote, resulting in the first pro-Kurdish quasi-faction in parliament since 1991.[5]

Given that the two-thirds parliamentary majority required for constitutional amendments lay beyond its reach, many centrist observers hoped the AKP would refocus its agenda on a national consensus favoring democratic reform and economic growth. Such centrist hopes focused in particular on a compromise candidate for president. Instead, the AKP, undaunted by its loss of seats, emphasized its 13-percentage point increase in the popular vote, interpreting that as a mandate to consolidate its political power and please its Islamist base. The AKP renewed its push for Abdullah Gül's candidacy for president in an election scheduled one month after the parliamentary election.

Throughout the first half of August, the secular camp hoped that the CHP, with MHP as a new parliamentary partner, would again use the procedural tactic of boycotting a parliamentary vote on the presidential election of Gül to block a quorum. But the national mood had shifted since spring. More Turks now objected to the general staff's electronic memorandum as inappropriate interference in Turkish politics. In addition, nationalist sentiment had continued to grow, with members of all political camps interpreting a range of U.S. and European actions (some of which are discussed in Chapter 5) as directed against Turkey. The growth in nationalism led many voters on the right, who embraced traditional Islam as a key element in Turkish identity, to seek a "devout Muslim" president. After failing to garner a majority on August 23, Abdullah Gül was elected president in the second round, on August 28, capping a mid-summer surge in support for the AKP.[6]

Presidential and Court Victories Embolden the AKP

With Gül's election, leaders of a single political party with an Islamist past secured Turkey's three key offices (president, prime minister, and speaker of parliament) for the first time since the foundation of the republic. Turkey's supporters in the West (once again) hoped the AKP government would use its strengthened political capital to re-energize democratizing reforms required for EU accession. Instead, Prime Minister Erdoğan quickly pressed for a constitutional amendment to lift the headscarf ban.

The headscarf issue continues to carry tremendous political and social significance in Turkey. Although many Turkish women from conservative backgrounds embrace the scarf as a religious requirement and an instrument of partial liberation from being treated as sexual objects, many others fear that social and political pressure to don the scarf will undermine their personal freedoms and gender equality. Conflicting tensions over the scarf are embodied in the wives of the prime minister and president, Emine Erdoğan and Hayrünnisa Gül, whose families compelled them to wear it.[7]

In January 2008, the AKP scored a crucial political and legal victory by securing a parliamentary approval of the constitutional amendments required to overturn the ban on headscarf in universities. The party's opponents counterattacked. In March 2008, the chief prosecutor of the High Appeals Court, Abdurrahman Yalçinkaya, a staunch Kemalist, brought a case to the Constitutional Court charging the AKP and its leaders with being "a focal point of efforts to change the secular nature of the Republic." He argued that the AKP should be disbanded and 71 of its leaders (including President Gül and Prime Minister Erdoğan) banned from politics.

The court deliberated this landmark case for several months. In June 2008, before deciding the AKP's fate, the judges ended the headscarf debate—at least for the time being—by ruling that the amendments allowing university women to wear the scarf on university property violated the constitutional principle of secularism.

That decision was a serious defeat for the AKP. It fueled public perceptions that a subsequent court ruling would close down the party and end its leaders' participation in politics. The AKP and its supporters responded with a public campaign portraying the Constitutional Court heading toward a "judicial coup." Such accusations resonated in the EU and United States, where officials and analysts believed that the banning of the country's most popular political party would weaken Turkish democracy.

At the same time, the AKP administration launched an investigation into alleged plots by a group of retired generals and other Kemalist allies in and out of government in what became known as the "Ergenekon" case (see Chapter 4). Societal tension increased, and pressure built on the judges from all directions. Even some of the AKP's opponents worried that, if banned from politics, the party's leaders would return even stronger; that had happened with Erbakan and Erdoğan. Others feared that shuttering the AKP itself would prompt political instability that could undermine the economy and fuel a new financial crisis.

The Constitutional Court reached its historic decision in July 2008, ruling against closing the AKP by only a seven to six margin. But the court, terming the AKP a "hub of anti-secular activities," also reduced its state subsidy. The chairman of the court characterized this decision as "a serious warning," saying the AKP should "draw its own conclusions" about the consequences of violating secular principles. As newspaper columnist Soli Özel, put it, "The AKP is on probation. . . . The court clearly said it sees the party as a focal institution for Islamizing the country."[8]

But the AKP saw the outcome differently—as it was the first time a Turkish Islamist party had survived a concerted effort by the Kemalist establishment to shut it down. The AKP thus felt emboldened to pursue a more aggressive agenda to restore a broader Islamic role in Turkish society and determination of Turkish identity.

The central, enduring tension between secularism and democracy had again been laid bare, and there was no use trying to finesse or conceal it. The Kemalists were believers in modernism, as they reckoned it. The newly empowered Islamists pinned their hopes on the democratic process. The old facile assumption that democracy and secularism were inseparable twins was overtaken by the political changes that had settled upon Turkey.

In retrospect, the stewardship of Turgut Özal (first as prime minister, then president, from 1983 until his death a decade later) may well have presented a rare chance to bridge Turkey's secularist-religious divide. He was both a man of Turkey's conservative heartland and a worldly politician who sought for the nation's membership in the European Union and who did much to bring the Kurds into the mainstream of political life. His brand of Islam was moderate, at its core the kind of faith with which most Turks feel at ease.

Özal had made his way around the Kemalist inheritance, amending and updating it without triggering a backlash from its adherents. His premature death robbed his country of the chance to reconcile the two camps competing for its direction and identity. In the decade that followed him, the country would witness greater polarization. Where Özal smothered differences, the Islamists and their secularist rivals would sharpen them with increasing force and conviction.

CHAPTER FOUR

Reshaping Identity by Restoring Islam

Emboldened by its political and legal victories, the AKP intensified what many of its opponents have called a cultural counter-revolution to reshape the Turkish identity and undo the Kemalist inheritance itself.

In launching his radical reforms, Mustafa Kemal introduced the principle of *revolutionism*, according to which the Turkish government would carry out a complete and revolutionary transformation of society through Westernization and modernization. In Kemal's view, because "every society has a collective idea . . . true revolutionaries are those who know how to discover the real preferences in the spirits and consciousness of people whom they want to lead to a revolution of progress and renovation."[1] Thus "the function of the revolutionaries" was to discover this "collective idea" of society and guide society's members toward achieving it. This, according to Atatürk, required that political leaders not only respond to society's diverse demands but also shape those demands on the basis of an enlightened vision of the nation's interests.[2]

After winning the presidential and parliamentary elections and surviving an effort to close down their party, AKP leaders had reason to believe that the "spirits and consciousness" of the people to which Atatürk had referred now favored a cultural counter-revolution that would return Islam to a more prominent role in Turkish society. Polling data on societal attitudes reinforced this perception. The Pew Global Attitudes Project reported in October 2007 that Turkish public support for a secular state dropped from 73 percent in 2002 to 55 percent in 2007, while TESEV, a prominent Turkish NGO, found that the number of Turks indentifying themselves primarily as Muslims (as opposed to as Turkish citizens or according to their ethnic identity) increased from 36 percent in 1999 to 46 percent in 2006.

The AKP government viewed its political-legal victories and the social trends noted above as a mandate to shore up its political strength and advance its cultural counter-revolution. The AKP's growing strength derived from their leaders' success in tapping into popular sentiment that favored restoration of Islam's societal role, as Turks grew weary of the corruption and stale ideology that characterized the secular political parties. But the leaders were also using their political power to reshape popular attitudes to clear the way for further Islamization. The AKP realized that to succeed in restoring Islam's influence in shaping Turkish life, it would first have to neutralize its secular political opponents.

Consolidating Power by Controlling the Media

The AKP government began to attack its secular opponents shortly after winning the November 2002 election, focusing on those who controlled major media outlets that could shape societal attitudes and demands. In early 2004, the government prosecuted several members of Istanbul's Uzan family, which had massive media holdings and was widely seen as one of Turkey's most corrupt business conglomerates. (The American telecommunications giant Motorola had sued the Uzan business empire for allegedly embezzling $4.5 billion.) The Uzans had enjoyed relative impunity from prosecution under previous Turkish governments, whose leaders feared retaliation by family patriarchs; in the past, they had reportedly threatened their enemies with financial ruin and physical harm. Many secular Turks and Americans cheered the AKP's courage in dismantling the Uzan empire.

By hindsight, the government also appears to have had a political motivation. One of the family's leaders, Cem Uzan, formed a new political party (named "Genç," or "Youth"), which mounted a serious challenge to the AKP in the 2002 parliamentary elections. During the election campaign, the Uzans' *Star* newspaper published a provocative photo of Erdoğan, taken several years earlier when he was mayor of Istanbul, kneeling before the Afghan warlord and Taliban leader Gulbuddin Hekmatyar. After the election, though his Genç Party did not win enough votes to enter parliament, Cem Uzan retained strong popularity. Erdoğan publicly expressed concern about Uzan's political staying power, noting "Our only competition is the Genç Party."[3] In response to these fears, the AKP launched an investigation that eventually produced arrest warrants for Cem Uzan and several other family members (who remain at large), and transferred ownership of the newspaper to political allies.

The AKP's political motivation in restricting media ownership was also evident in the government's 2007 intervention in the sale of the *Sabah*-ATV group, then Turkey's second-largest media group. In April 2007, the government's Savings and Deposit Insurance Fund seized control of the bankrupt group and transferred ownership to the Çalık Group, a large and respected conglomerate. Çalık has a strong interest in major energy projects that require governmental support; moreover, Prime Minister Erdoğan's son-in-law, Berat Albayrak, is a Çalık general manager. The prime minister reportedly stepped in to force the withdrawal of all competing bidders; state bank governors were fired after objecting to loans offered to finance the sale as violations of state banking regulations. Following this transaction, *Sabah*-ATV's coverage shifted from neutral to strongly pro-government.

The AKP's success in gaining influence—if not control—over *Sabah*-ATV seemed to embolden it to target one of its most powerful critics, the Doğan Media Group. Turkey's largest media holding company, Doğan owns outlets that claim half of the country's print and broadcast media market share; they include a partnership with CNN for a 24-hour Turkish-language news channel, CNN Türk.

The Doğan Media Group drew the government's ire by extensively covering several scandals involving the AKP. The most prominent of them surrounds the *Deniz Feneri* (Lighthouse) Islamic charity, which is based in Germany. A German court in 2008 accused Zahid Akman, a close associate of Prime Minister Erdoğan and then-President of the Supreme Board of Radio and Television Commission, which supervises all Turkish radio and TV broadcasts, of transferring tens of millions of euros between *Deniz Feneri's* offices in Germany and pro-AKP television channel *Kanal 7* in Turkey. When Doğan's flagship newspaper, *Hürriyet,* reported that "Erdoğan's name was indirectly implicated and persons close to him directly accused of wrongdoing" in the *Deniz Feneri* case, the prime minister reacted by accusing Doğan Chairman Aydın Doğan, one of Turkey's most prominent business leaders, of conducting a "systematic defamation campaign" against him. Erdoğan was so angry that he advised Turks to boycott Doğan's newspapers.

Another major corruption case covered by the Doğan media outlets involved AKP Deputy Chairman Şaban Dişli, who was accused of taking $1 million in exchange for facilitating a change in an Istanbul zoning permit to allow a company in which he previously was a partner to construct a building. Dişli ultimately resigned as a result of the Doğan media coverage of extensive corruption allegations leveled by the chairman of the CHP Parliamentary Group.

The AKP government responded by escalating its confrontation with the Doğan group beyond tough statements by Prime Minister Erdoğan. In February 2009, the government slapped the group with a tax penalty of $408 million and followed up in August with a fine of $2.5 billion for allegedly unpaid taxes. A favorable ruling by the appellate court will likely drive the company out of business. As of January 2010, the Doğan group appeared to be buckling under this government pressure, and even willing to sell several of its key media holdings to AKP allies.

Whether the AKP intends these penalties to be a way of silencing, punishing, or gaining control of the Doğan group remains to be seen. What is clear is that such enormous tax fines have a stifling impact on the media; the European Commission noted, in its October 2009 progress report on Turkey's EU accession effort, that "The high fines imposed by the revenue authority potentially undermine the economic viability of the group and therefore affect freedom of the press in practice."

The Ergenekon Investigation: Silencing Opponents through the Courts

The AKP's success in the Uzan case and its battle against the Doğan Media Group were salvos in its battle to subdue previously untouchable secular opponents, including the military. Following its victory in the 2007 elections, the AKP government capitalized on its growing political strength to use the legal system to launch a similar but more controversial effort. As the Constitutional Court's deliberations began on whether to close the AKP, the police discovered weapons caches in Istanbul. The ministry of justice launched an investigation into an alleged conspiracy involving former high-ranking military officers and civilians to overthrow the government. The purported conspirators were alleged to belong to the "Deep State," a loose grouping of secular leaders who were believed to be resorting to anti-constitutional methods to counter what they deemed to be threats to the state.

The ministry of justice dubbed the alleged conspirators the "Ergenekon" group, a name stemming from the legendary Ergenekon in the Altai Mountains of Central Asia. According to myth, a grey she-wolf led the tribe that became the Turkish nation on its westward migrations from the Ergenekon Valley through dangerous mountain passes. This mythological wolf and her valley became powerful symbols of nationalism, inspiring a deep pride in modern Turks' connections to their Turkic ancestors. Turkey's secular political parties, especially those on the right, have historically used this myth to rally popular support. The AKP now seemed to be appropriating this tale to shore up its own political agenda.

At the outset of the Ergenekon investigation, few Turks objected to a government effort to prosecute genuine criminals, especially those who might have been conspiring to launch another military coup. Thanks to the 1996 case of the car accident in Susurluk (discussed in Chapter 2), it was widely assumed that shady characters sometimes worked with former and current state officials to take the law into their own hands while pursuing political objectives, a practice often described in such reassuring phrases as "safeguarding secular democracy." (Before the Ergenekon investigation had begun, coup planning within the military appears to have been stopped by senior officers.)

But the fact that the Ergenekon investigation coincided with the Constitutional Court's case on the AKP's closure raised suspicions that the trial might be politically and ideologically driven. Many Turks began to worry about an ideological reorientation of the case as the investigation's pool of suspects broadened well beyond those associated with the so-called Deep State. In the summer of 2008, university rectors, journalists, and civil-society activists, who had nothing in common other than their desire to defend secular democratic values, were arrested, questioned, and in some cases detained for months without charges. The leftist and secular *Cumhuriyet* suffered in particular; both its editor and its Ankara bureau chief were arrested. Other journalists who expressed anti-Islamist and anti-AKP sentiments were pressured into silence through threats of possible indictments with relation to the Ergenekon investigation.

Thousands of other avowed opponents of Islamism feared that the AKP government had launched a campaign to intimidate them by tapping their telephones. Such fears were fed by disclosures in AKP-allied newspapers of private (and often embarrassing) phone conversations. In response to these fears, the minister of communications brazenly said, "If you do not want people to know what you are saying, don't speak on the phone."[4] He added, "If you do not have anything to hide, you should not be concerned about wiretaps." Deniz Baykal, the leader of the opposition CHP, characterized such tactics as designed to "create an empire of fear."[5]

Public opinion moved sharply against the Ergenekon investigation in April 2009, following the raid on the Foundation for the Support of Modern Life (known by the Turkish acronym ÇYDD). The foundation helps girls from poor and conservative families get an education through scholarships provided by its "Father, Send Me to School" campaign. The foundation also plays an indispensable role in securing permission from fathers for their daughters to attend elementary and secondary schools in rural and underdeveloped regions of Turkey.

ÇYDD's founder, Türkan Saylan, had devoted her life to advancing secular education in Turkey. She participated in the 2007 rallies, promoting the slogan "No coup, no *sharia.*" When the police raided her house as part of the Ergenekon investigation, Saylan was 73 years old and battling terminal cancer. She died shortly afterwards, and her funeral attracted tens of thousands of supporters who bristled at her arrest and the government's harassment of her foundation.[6]

Still, the police proceeded with tracking down nearly 15,000 girls attending school on ÇYDD scholarships, and investigated them for potential involvement in "terrorist activities." The CHP leader Baykal assailed the raids, charged that the government aimed to "prevent anybody from supporting modern education . . . [especially] sending girls to school . . ." Baykal further accused the AKP government of trying to make it "a crime to support education that is not under the control of religious sects."[7]

The Ergenekon investigation has grown so broad that the indictment runs for thousands of pages. It is filled with innuendo, rumors, unfounded speculation, and logical contradictions, leading many Turkish observers to conclude that the effort has evolved into a campaign against the AKP's political and ideological opponents. Further support for this argument was provided by a pro-Gülen prosecutor's decision in February 2010 to arrest a fellow prosecutor in Erzincan for participation in the Ergenekon scandal—after he had investigated Islamist educational and fundraising activities of the ultra-conservative Ismailağa *tariqa* and the Gülen movement.

Shaping an Openly Islamist Identity

The Uzan, Doğan, and Ergenekon cases suggest that the AKP government is using legal tools to counter its political opponents and intimidate them into silence. Such an approach would help the party cement and deepen its political strength. With its political opponents weakened and silenced and with media outlets increasingly in its grip, the AKP would have cleared the way to consolidate its political and legal power. Perhaps more profoundly, it would also be able to advance its social agenda, which evolved within Erbakan's various parties, to Islamize Turkish society in a cultural counter-revolution.

Additional evidence of the AKP's attempt to harness the media to restore Islam's societal role emerged in 2005, when the AKP-dominated parliament elected a conservative director, Zahid Akman, to the powerful Supreme Board of Radio and Television Commission; the board members then elected him president. Under Akman's leadership, the commission has presided over an increase in state TV and radio programs that promote conservative values, knowledge of Islam, and Muslim heritage under the Ottoman Empire.

Anti-Semitism, a core element of Islamist ideology around the globe, has also crept into state TV broadcasts in Turkey. During Israel's war with Lebanon in the summer of 2006, the state-run Turkish Radio and Television dropped the Roman Polanski movie, *The Pianist*, depicting a Jewish pianist's life in Nazi-occupied Warsaw, from its programming after complaints from Islamists that the movie portrayed Jews as victims rather than oppressors. In the fall of 2009, Turkish Radio and Television aired a prime-time TV drama, *Ayrılık* ("Separation"), which one-sidedly depicted Israeli soldiers shooting at Palestinian children and mistreating elderly Arabs—in spite of Israel's diplomatic protests that such harsh portrayals of Israeli soldiers were distorted, unfair, and dangerous. Such slanted depictions continued into early 2010, precipitating a near diplomatic collapse between the governments of Turkey and Israel.

Outside the state's broadcast services, the AKP works in union with private media outlets to promote Islamic values. The government enjoys strong and consistent support from the *Star* newspaper, which the AKP encouraged its allies to acquire after dismantling the Uzan conglomerate in 2004. Another private daily newspaper, *Yeni Şafak*, serves as the party's de facto mouthpiece. The son of *Yeni Şafak*'s owner is Berat Albayrak, Prime Minister Erdoğan's son-in-law.

The AKP's agenda also enjoys a continuous and strong boost from the Gülen movement's media outlets, especially its influential flagship newspaper, *Zaman* (which also publishes an English edition), and its Samanyolu TV station. The defense and intelligence journal *Jane's* described the relationship between the AKP and the Fethullah Gülen community as "a symbiotic co-existence."[8] Accordingly, the AKP provided key bureaucratic positions to members of the Gülen movement, including in law enforcement and intelligence agencies. In return, Gülen's cadres have deflected pressure from the secular establishment on the party at key moments (as during the party closure case in 2007).

Intelligence leaks involving top echelons of the Turkish military and judiciary, especially for the Ergenekon investigation, have usually appeared first in *Taraf*, an independent leftist newspaper whose editors share with the Gülen movement a common enmity towards the Turkish military. The leaks often move from *Taraf* to *Zaman* and other newspapers owned by the Gülen movement. *Taraf* has repeatedly published allegations of military plotting against the AKP government and Gülen movement at tense moments when the party's political opponents appeared to be on the rise, such as following the AKP's disappointing election results in the March 2009 local elections and Western criticism that fall of the tax penalty imposed against the Doğan group.

The Gülen movement's impact in generating a cultural counter-revolution extends well beyond its own media outlets and those of its ally, *Taraf*. Large numbers of Gülen's followers have secured key positions throughout the bureaucracy, especially in the national police. Meanwhile, the AKP government has helped the movement broaden its joint operations with schools, boarding homes, and lucrative businesses such as Bank Asya, which provides interest-free Islamic banking. These companies, along with others controlled by conservative Muslim owners, have merged under the Gülen organization's Turkish Industrialists Confederation (TUSKON). That organization's members accompany the prime minister and president on their official foreign trips; and they have used their TUSKON network and its ties to the government to secure trade and investment privileges in foreign countries ranging from Africa to East Asia. The Gülen movement's reach is becoming global, with secondary schools in Central and South Asia, Africa, Europe, and the United States, as well as a think-tank in Washington, D.C. (the Rumi Forum) and several Turkish studies programs at prestigious American universities.

In sum, the Gülen movement aims to transcend the themes of spirituality, tolerance, and compatibility of Islam and the West that dominate Fethullah Gülen's writings. The movement's underlying, eventual goal, like that of other Islamist organizations, appears to be replacing values of secular democracy that now govern societies in Turkey and other countries with large Muslim populations with values defined by Islam.

The most important component of the movement's efforts to advance Islamism is education. Its network of secondary schools follows a secular curriculum but promotes conservative religious norms outside the classroom, especially in dormitories. In an extensive study for the Open Society Institute in 2008, prominent social scientist Binnaz Toprak reported that the Gülen-school dormitories (known as "Houses of Light") seem to be the loci of religious indoctrination. According to Toprak, religious instruction regularly takes place there after school hours, with emphasis given to restoring Islam's proper role throughout society. Behavior normal among adolescents in a secular society, but discouraged by Islamists, is banned inside the Houses of Light, including males socializing with females, members of either sex viewing non-Islamic TV stations, and female students wearing pants.

Gülen's secondary schools and Houses of Light are a midpoint in the movement's effort to promote Islamization in the lives of Turkish students. Prior to students entering these schools, the Gülen movement identifies those from rural families with modest incomes, and gives them free tutoring at a network of learning centers. These students then enter Gülen's secondary schools. Upon graduation, they receive a free education (including all living expenses) at universities, all covered by the movement. After they graduate from university, the movement helps them secure jobs, often in prestigious sectors of the state bureaucracy. The movement is also said to arrange marriages for young men.[9]

Echoing those efforts, the AKP government is using education to promote conservative Islamic values. Since coming to power in November 2002, the party has expanded Turkey's state system of religious schools, which historically have operated separately from the state-run secular schools. Between 2002 and 2008, the AKP doubled the number of Qur'an schools, to which parents voluntarily send children to memorize the Qur'an (as in *madrassas* in many Islamic countries). Unlike in the past, students as young as ten are now encouraged to attend these schools. A large majority of those who do are female.[10]

Similarly, between 2002 and 2007, the AKP government presided over a doubling of İmam Hatip schools, religious secondary schools designed to train *imams* and *hatips*. The İmam Hatip (IH) curriculum promotes the elevation of pan-Islamism as a core element of the Turkish identity. In contrast to Turkey's secular schools, IH students memorize large segments of the Qur'an and learn conservative interpretations of Sunni Islam. Many female students are also encouraged to defy the legal ban against wearing the Islamic headscarf in state schools.

The yearly total of IH graduates far exceeds the number of annual job openings for *imams* and *hatips*. Moreover, as with the large number of female graduates of Qur'an schools, more than 60 percent of IH graduates are now female, even though no women are allowed to take the jobs for which they have been trained. The AKP's encouragement of girls to attend Qur'an and IH schools suggests a desire on the part of the party to spread Islamic values to girls who would otherwise receive a secular education. (Without the possibility of working as *imams* or *hatips*, these girls would presumably obtain jobs elsewhere and convey Islamic ideals in the workforce and/or become mothers and raise the next generation according to Islamic norms.)

The large disparity between students training to become *imams* and *hatips* and the number of available positions indicates that the İmam Hatip schools are being used to advance the broader social agenda of reshaping Turkish society. A 2008 RAND report on the growth of political Islam in Turkey points out that "the AKP government has been placing İmam-

Hatip graduates in government departments and state-owned firms at all levels of responsibility. . . . [T]he progressive introduction of AKP cadres, including *İmam-Hatip* graduates, into the state apparatus may be one of the leading vehicles for change in the secular-religious balance over time."[11]

The AKP has complemented this expansion of Turkey's system of religious schools with programs designed to instill Islamic norms in the state's secular schools—marking the first time in the history of the republic that secular schools have emphasized such values. Previously, religious education in state schools was limited to a few hours of classroom teaching each week, focusing on (Sunni) Islamic ethics and principles. Today, a rising number of teachers in the state schools nudge students to perform daily prayers at school, organize Islamic celebrations, and promote Islamic values in social studies classes.

More revealing still, public schools in Anatolia increasingly suspend classes during Friday prayer hours. Makeshift mosques are now common in schools across that region; in the southeastern town of Batman, administrators, teachers, and students pray together in improvised mosques in science laboratories. A religious holiday that commemorates the Prophet Muhammad's birth is now widely celebrated in many parts of Turkey under directions from various ministries, with girls aged between seven and ten covered from head to toe in the Islamic veil. Guides for high school philosophy courses propagate religious values, with teachers expected to teach students the value of religion and the existence of God.[12] When asked why they are departing from the traditional norms of Turkey's state schools, most teachers explain that they are afraid of being fired, transferred, or not getting promoted if a superior notices their absence during prayers. (Although such incidents—when publicized by the media—lead to strong reaction from the Kemalist establishment and civil society, and even from some in the AKP, these practices continue with little oversight—not surprising, given that the ministry of education is under AKP rule.)

In addition, there are growing indications that under the AKP, scientific learning, a key foundation of the Turkish republic's education system since its establishment, is being given a religious focus. After decades of teaching evolution, public schools are now required to teach creationism as well. The head of the Scientific and Technological Research Council of Turkey, who reports to the government, fired the respected editor of Turkey's *Science and Technology* magazine in 2009 in reaction to her plan to publish a cover story commemorating Darwin's 200th birthday. Intellectuals allied with the AKP, such as Islamic sect leader Adnan Oktar (also known as Harun Yahya), are promoting creationism *over* evolution.

As *The Washington Post* reported, Oktar calls Darwin "the worst Fascist there has ever been." This assault on scientific thinking has had a pronounced impact within Turkey: a 2008 survey in the American journal *Science* found that *fewer than 25 percent of Turks accepted evolution, by far the lowest percentage of any developed nation.*[13]

The advance of Islam into secular education appears to be part of a broader trend under the AKP government to soften the separation of religion from the activities of the state. As noted in Chapter 2, Atatürk established the Directorate of Religious Affairs (or the *Diyanet*) to separate mosque and state. His underlying goal was to prevent a narrow interpretation of Islam and the legal system of *sharia* from dictating social norms in Turkish society, including in private life. According to the 1924 Law on the Directorate of Religious Affairs, secular laws promulgated by Turkey's parliament replaced norms of governance previously based on *sharia,* while the *Diyanet* acquired an advisory role on issues concerning faith and worship. The *Diyanet*'s specific functions were limited to the administration of mosques and the training and supervision of *muftis* (religious scholars who offer opinions on Islamic matters and administer religious services) and *imams.* In this way, the *Diyanet* became a key element in the Turkish government's effort to maintain separation of mosque and state.

In recent years, however, the *Diyanet* has strayed beyond this narrow scope of activities, and begun to convey Islamic norms into private life on behalf of the state. Evidence of that popped up during a January 2008 interview on a private TV news network with *Diyanet* President Ali Bardakoğlu, who stressed that wearing the headscarf was "an obligation incumbent on all Muslim women." This venture into dictating social norms for Turkish women marked a sharp departure for *Diyanet* chiefs, who had previously agreed with many Turkish theologians that the headscarf is a cultural tradition but not a religious requirement. A few months after Bardakoğlu's comments, *Diyanet*'s website featured a series of online publications that warned women to stay away from perfumes and clothes that reveal their "adornments and figure," and advised that it is a sin for women to stimulate men sexually (which also meant it was the responsibility of women to cover themselves properly).[14] The *Diyanet* has also distributed pamphlets for women on marriage, sexuality, and duties as a proper housewife.[15]

Such apparent efforts by the Turkish government to dictate social norms to women on the basis of Islam are having a significant and negative impact on one of the greatest achievements of Atatürk's reforms, gender equality. As noted in Chapter 1, Atatürk made equal rights for women a top priority of his secular cultural revolution. His reforms freed them from the strictures imposed by *sharia* during the Ottoman Empire, providing women with new rights and opportunities, including the right to vote at a time when there was no women's suffrage in much of the West.

In recent years, such monumental progress in securing the rights of Turkish women has begun to weaken. As a recent United Nations study by one of Turkey's most prominent social scientists, Yeşim Arat, shows, there is "propagation of patriarchal religious values that sanction secondary roles for women, both through public bureaucracy, the educational system, and civil society organizations. Party cadres with sexist values are infiltrating the political system, and religious movements that were once banned are establishing schools, dormitories, and off-campus Qur'an schools which socialize the young into religiously sanctioned secondary roles for women."[16]

As AKP leaders advocate the reintroduction of Islamic norms into daily life, countless women are altering the way they lead their own lives. The number wearing the headscarf has increased significantly during the AKP government. Respected pollster Tarhan Erdem found in a 2007 survey that the number of scarf-wearing women in Turkey increased nearly fivefold during the period of 2003 to 2007 from 4.1 percent to 19.7 percent. The percentage of married women wearing the scarf tripled during the same period—to 75 percent. This latter statistic suggests that many women cover their heads, especially in urban areas, in response to pressure from conservative husbands. Hayrünnisa Gül, the wife of President Gül, donned the scarf and quit high school when, at age 15, she wed her 30-year-old husband in an arranged marriage. Zeynep Babacan, the wife of Deputy Prime Minister Ali Babacan, was a university student when she married her husband in an arranged marriage, and immediately donned the headscarf and quit her studies.

Many other AKP leaders' wives have similar stories.[17] Broader social pressures in Islamist circles also compel girls to wear the scarf long before marriage. Emine Erdoğan, the wife of Prime Minister Erdoğan, has spoken of being forced to wear one when she turned 15, noting, "When my older brother told me that from now on I had to cover myself, I even considered suicide."[18] Before covering, she was attending a school of arts and was passionate about women's fashion; after she donned the scarf, she quit school.

Recent studies indicate this period of increased headscarf wearing coincides with a decrease in the quality of life of

Turkish women, especially with regard to gender equality. Since its inception in 2006, the World Economic Forum's Global Gender Gap report has shown continuing backsliding in Turkey. By 2009, Turkey ranked *129th* out of a total of 134 countries in terms of allocating equal resources and opportunities to men and women, placing Turkey lower than Iran and Oman and nearly as low as Saudi Arabia, Pakistan, and Yemen.

(Turkey also ranked 130th—fourth from last—in female economic participation and opportunity, 119th in female enrollment in secondary education, 110th in equality of educational attainment, 107th in political empowerment, and 93rd in equality of health care and survival. Almost all African countries have higher political empowerment for women, and all West European countries rank in the top 20.)

This erosion in gender equality in Turkey plays out in the workforce. According to a 2009 report by the World Bank and Turkey's State Planning Organization, "While the share of women participating in the labor force has risen since the 1980s in countries with a similar starting point, it has fallen considerably in Turkey—from 34.3 percent in 1988 to 21.6 percent in 2008." The report further notes that in 2006, Turkey had fewer women participating in its economy than any other country that is a member of the Organization for Economic Cooperation and Development (OECD) or is located in Europe or Central Asia.[19] According to a report by the Turkish Enterprise and Business Confederation, during 2003–2007, despite an average growth rate of 6.5 percent in Turkey's GNP and an increase in its overall employment rate of 1.1 percent, the rate of women's employment *decreased* by 0.8 percent.[20] These data indicate that social pressures, rather than economic factors, are driving Turkish women away from the workforce.

Gender equality is also ebbing in Turkish politics. When women obtained the right to vote in 1934, only 16 other countries already permitted it. The next year, eighteen women were elected to parliament, constituting 4.6 percent of all deputies, which ranked Turkey second in the world in terms of percentage of female parliamentarians. In 1999, women held twenty-three seats in the Turkish parliament, and in 2002, this number increased by one. Today, under the AKP's leadership, only nine deputies of the parliament are women. Moreover, there is not a single woman among eighty-one provincial governors, and only fifteen among 900 heads of regional districts, while only two of Turkey's 81 cities have female mayors.[21]

This weakening of eight-plus decades of progress on gender equality has been accompanied by de facto application of Islamic *sharia* norms in the treatment of women and girls at home, especially in rural areas and municipalities. Numerous newspaper reports indicate an increase in child marriages and polygamy. (No comprehensive study has yet been done.) One prominent Islamic businessman has argued in favor of polygamy, claiming there would be no prostitution if it were possible to have multiple wives.

Even more disturbingly, when Hüseyin Üzmez, a well-known writer at the Islamist daily *Vakit,* was arrested for sexually molesting a fourteen-year-old girl, many of his Islamist supporters came to his defense, arguing that he may have "married" the victim beforehand, in keeping with *sharia* norms. The ministry of justice's Institute of Forensic Medicine concluded the child victim suffered no psychological damage from the assault. With the secular press keeping the story alive and women's organizations and secular doctors pursuing the case, Üzmez was finally convicted of rape and sentenced to 13 years in prison.

When confronted with statistics on decreasing gender equality, many AKP leaders routinely argue that such data reflect social forces to which the party is reacting rather than driving. But rarely, if ever, do the leaders decry these worrying trends or offer policy steps to reverse them. On the contrary, many aggravate the weakening of gender equality through their public statements. For example, Finance Minister Mehmet Şimşek blamed women's quests for jobs as aggravating an increase in unemployment during the economic downturn of 2008–2009.[22] As mentioned above, the *Diyanet* now promotes *sharia* norms in de facto fashion by discouraging women from using perfume outside their homes and from remaining alone with a man who is not a relative.[23] The UN study prepared by Yeşim Arat suggests that if this approach continues, it could have a devastating impact on women's equality in the workplace: "If the *Diyanet* argues women should not remain alone with men, the pious Prime Minister would have no incentive to provide opportunities to women for employment."

In addition to the *Diyanet*, the AKP supporters in virtually all state bureaucracies advocate gender inequality. Arat's UN study mentions that male supporters of the party are "uncomfortable in working with women in public service. . . . AKP bureaucrats and politicians did not merely treat women administrators with traditional patriarchal attitudes, but they also resented the presence of women without headscarves in public spaces." Top AKP officials have advocated that Turkish women withdraw from the workforce to pursue societal roles deemed appropriate by Islamist standards; Prime Minister Erdoğan has stated repeatedly that women should focus on having three babies. Municipal governments routinely distribute pamphlets encouraging women to be subservient to their husbands.

As with gender inequality, AKP's pro-Islamic advocacy is aggravating intolerance towards religious minorities. Jews have been targeted in particular, despite Turkey's generally positive record in respecting the rights of its Jewish community. Anti-Semitic propaganda has been growing since the early days of the AKP government. Hitler's *Mein Kampf* became a bestseller in 2005; the editions sold in Turkey lacked the introduction appearing in Western editions that explains the historical context and the horrors to which the manifesto helped lead. *The Protocols of the Elders of Zion*, a Czarist Russian hoax describing a Jewish plan to achieve global domination (and claiming Jews use children's blood to make matzo), is also widely read as truthful. Both of these books have been published in large printings and sold at subsidized prices; while it is not clear who pays the subsidies, the AKP did not discourage the books' wide dissemination nor make an effort to dispel their hateful messages.

Popular anti-Semitism has been driven by the AKP government's harsh attacks on Israel, marking a sharp departure from the strategic partnership Turkey established with Israel in the 1990s. Prime Minister Erdoğan accused Israel of "crimes against humanity" in 2009 in connection with that nation's attacks on Palestinians in Gaza. At the World Economic Forum in Davos in January of that year, Erdoğan insulted Israeli President Shimon Peres in a tirade against Israel, claiming, "You [Israelis] know very well how to kill." Soon thereafter, following an Israeli raid on Gaza, the Turkish Ministry of National Education made an unprecedented gesture by encouraging all public schools to hold a minute of silence to reflect solidarity with the Palestinians; never before had Turkish secular schools been encouraged to express support for another nation. In early February, Istanbul's municipal government (headed by the AKP) opened in the city's busiest metro station an exhibit of cartoons depicting bloodthirsty Israelis killing Palestinians, with one satanic Israeli soldier washing his hands with blood from a faucet labeled "the United States."[24]

Such propaganda has generated a wave of anti-Semitism in Turkey, a country in which discrimination against Jews had been latent yet socially unacceptable. Anti-Semitism is now reaching alarming levels. In 2008, 76 percent of Turks viewed Jews negatively, while only 7 percent expressed favorable opinions.[25] Leyla Navaro, one of the country's most prominent psychologists and a professor at the prestigious Bosphorus University, and member of Turkey's Jewish community, warned in an op-ed in the liberal daily *Radikal* that she sensed an unprecedented level of anti-Semitism in Turkey: "I feel worried, sad and scared for myself and for my country's future, which is leaning towards racism."[26]

Growing anti-Semitism is driving increasing numbers of Turkish Jews to immigrate to Israel. In an interview with NTV in January 2010, Eyal Peretz, the head of the Turkish Jews' Society in Israel, said that over the past ten years, an average of 60 Jews emigrated from Turkey to Israel but that in 2009, the number increased tenfold. He said the main reasons for the migration were the "disillusionment" of Jews living in Turkey, "anti-Jewish" rallies in the country, "the burning of Israeli flags in Istanbul," "the Turkish PM calling Turkey's Jews 'guests,' in their own country," and "other rising anti-Jewish developments."

Turkey's Christian minorities are also feeling increasing social pressure. Turkish sociologist Binnaz Toprak noted in her report that the number of professing Christians has diminished significantly in Anatolia following the killing of a Roman Catholic priest in Trabzon in 2006, murders of Christian missionaries in Malatya, and the stabbing of a Catholic priest in Izmir in 2007. According to Pew research in 2008, 52 percent of Turks had a negative view of Christians in 2004, and the number rose to 74 percent in 2008; of the populations surveyed, Turks had the least favorable views of Christians.

Turkey's largest Muslim minority, the Alevis, is also under pressure from the AKP's effort to elevate the societal role of conservative Sunnism. A blend of elements of Shia and Sunni Islam with other Anatolian religious and secular traditions, the ancient Alevi culture permits alcohol consumption and social interaction between men and women. Some policies of the AKP government seem to reflect a mistrust of Alevis, perhaps because the sect does not embrace the conservative interpretation of Sunnism that predominates within the AKP. Alevis complain that in their case, the government refuses to honor its own policy of promoting religious freedom; whereas the AKP encourages expanded mosque building to ensure that conservative Sunnis have places to worship according to their traditions, it presses Alevis to attend Sunni mosques rather than their own houses of worship (*cemevi*). Alevis also report discrimination in AKP-governed municipalities in terms of reduced access to government services.

Turkey's largest ethnic minority, the Kurds, has benefited from the AKP government's policies, specifically its initiative to restore the Kurdish community's cultural rights. European and U.S. leaders have praised government decisions in 2009 to allow TV broadcasts and school lessons in the Kurdish language, reflecting Prime Minister Erdoğan's statement four years earlier that "the solution to Turkey's Kurdish Problem is more democracy." When it comes to religion, however, the AKP encourages the Kurdish population—many of whom are Alevi—to demonstrate solidarity with Turkey's Sunni majority, in keeping with the earlier approach of Erbakan and his political parties.

Similar pressures impact the daily life of members of Turkey's Sunni majority. Reflecting its conservative interpretation of Sunni Islam, the AKP has reduced drinking by significantly increasing taxes on alcohol and sharply reducing the number of alcohol licenses issued to bars and restaurants. AKP authorities justify those restrictions with pretexts such as concerns that alcohol consumption disturbs the peace in residential areas, even when no residential dwellings are near the establishment in question. Following the AKP's lead, many municipal officials have banned alcohol at state-run restaurants and cafés, and some have suggested restricting its urban consumption to "drinking zones."

According to a survey by the Nielsen Corporation, the number of cafés, bars, and restaurants selling alcohol in Turkey decreased by 12 percent during 2005–2008.[27] According to Binnaz Toprak's study, the only restaurant in Kayseri (central Anatolia's largest city) that serves alcohol is located on the outskirts; the owner of a local café popular with young men and women told Toprak that his countless applications for an alcohol license have all been rejected. In such a climate, many Turks privately report they are shying away from drinking alcohol in public out of fear that their consumption might be reported by AKP supporters, jeopardizing jobs or prospective state contracts.

More broadly, those who ignore conservative Sunni norms in the workplace and in business worry that they are risking their professional and economic well-being. Government employees report their increasing fear that they are being monitored with regard to their outward expressions of Islamic piety. In September 2007, the Turkish daily *Milliyet* noted complaints of employees of the Turkish Electricity Distribution Company that the Ministry of Energy and Natural Resources requested the names of all employees who did not plan to fast during the holy month of Ramadan. Even government contracts are often awarded on the basis of expressions of religiosity by businessmen, especially on whether their wives wear headscarves.

Hüseyin Tuğcu, a founding AKP member, confirmed that bias, nonchalantly and without apology. It is normal, he said, for the wives of contractors working with the government to cover their heads to help their husbands secure government business: "If one wants to be successful, he must be flexible and ready to adapt to new circumstances. . . . If [he] wants to get the contract, he has to adjust and fix himself accordingly."[28]

Similarly, the AKP appears to offer preferential treatment in civil service hiring to outwardly pious, conservative Muslims. Toprak's research reports that appointees to key posts in local governments, school administrations, and hospitals are selected from the pro-AKP labor union Memur-Sen, whose membership ballooned during the seven years beginning in 2002 from 42,000 to 315,000 members. She (like many other researchers and journalists) also heard complaints from doctors, nurses, lawyers, and school teachers from different parts of Turkey that only people close to the AKP are promoted to executive levels in government.

In sum, the AKP government is generating cultural counter-revolution in response to the political and social norms that grew out of the revolutionary reforms implemented by Atatürk with the founding of the Turkish republic. The AKP's underlying goals seem to be to redefine the Turkish identity and social norms and mores by elevating the role of Islam vis-á-vis secularism. Although the party frames such policies as a response to social trends, the AKP is working actively to shape such trends through policies on education, civil service hiring, and government contracting. The discernible impacts on Turkish society include the weakening of gender equality, respect for religious minorities, and equal treatment in government hiring and contracting.

How these trends will play out remains unclear. In the past, Turkey's peculiar democratic system has maintained the separation of mosque and state, even when Islam reached a relative high point as a determinant of Turkish identity. But as the AKP chips away at institutions and norms established by Atatürk nearly 90 years ago, the society's readiness to swing back toward secularism may weaken.

What is clear is that the outcome of the struggle between the AKP and its secular opponents who are resisting Islamization may not be known for years. With the backfiring of the Turkish military's April 2007 "e-memorandum" and the decision of the constitutional court not to ban the AKP, the outcome of this struggle will in all likelihood be determined by Turkish voters rather than by legislative action, military fiat, or bureaucratic or judicial decrees. The party is preparing for this struggle by trying to silence its critics through control of media outlets and such intimidating steps as the Ergenekon investigation. The AKP's moves to bolster its political strength threaten to frustrate the hopes of millions of centrist voters who believed the party and the government it now controls would rejuvenate, not weaken, Turkish democracy.

This struggle does not occur in a global vacuum. When Kemalist secularism pushed Islam aside in the 1920s and 1930s, secularism was ascendant worldwide. Kemalism was but a variety of the secular, modernizing ideologies competing in the world stage—democratic liberalism, fascism, and Marxism. The global context is different today. The sacred has returned to international life. Religion makes political pronouncements more loudly and insistently and with greater confidence, and it is understandable that Turkey's Islamists believe that their aims and their momentum are at one with the winds blowing in other nations.

CHAPTER FIVE

The AKP's Foreign Policy

As Turks debate whether the AKP is Islamizing Turkish society to an unacceptable degree, they also argue over whether the party has deviated from the republic's traditional foreign policy orientation. From the 1950s until the end of the Cold War, Turkey took pride in serving as a key Euro-Atlantic ally that secured NATO's southern flank against Soviet expansion, while striving for full membership in the European Union. Many observers now believe Turkish foreign policy has shifted to a new "axis"—focused eastward and perhaps derivative of an Islamist agenda.[1] Current Turkish foreign policy, the AKP's domestic opponents argue, contradicts fundamental tenets laid down by Atatürk. Some Euro-Atlantic allies accuse Turkey of departing from years of shared approaches to Iran, Israel, and the broader Middle East; and they worry that Turkey is becoming "too Islamic" to be accepted as a full member of the EU.

The AKP rejects accusations that it has shifted Turkey's foreign policy axis. AKP leaders argue that changing international conditions allow Turkey to assert its leadership in its region and beyond, based on a proud historical legacy. In principle, the argument continues, Turkey's foreign policy remains consistent with Atatürk's core tenet of "peace at home, peace in the world"; what is new are additional elements based on fresh opportunities that arose with the end of the Cold War but do not contradict the fundamental values and interests of the Euro-Atlantic community. AKP leaders observe that the United States and other NATO allies look to Turkey as a key partner in resolving a broadening range of problems in Turkey's geo-strategic space.

In practice, it is evident that under the AKP, Turkish policies have changed with regard to several key issues on which Ankara and its Euro-Atlantic allies previously were aligned. What is less clear is whether such tactical changes reflect a fundamental strategic shift. Answering that question requires an exploration of the evolution of Turkish foreign policy since the founding of the republic in 1923.

Atatürk's Foreign Policy: Peace and the West

Mustafa Kemal's vision of how to interact with the rest of the world responded to the precarious security situation of the Turkish Republic at its birth. The European powers that had won the Great War in 1919 were eager to dismantle the Ottoman Empire and to bring its sprawling domains into their own spheres of influence. Against all odds, by 1923, the Turkish army Atatürk commanded had defeated the alliance of European powers and warded off their threat to the Turkish homeland.

Atatürk realized that to survive Turkey needed stability within its borders and in its geographical region. That led directly to his core concept of "peace at home, peace in the world." Atatürk's quest for domestic and regional peace generated a status quo mindset in foreign policy. Seeking to avoid risky conflicts that could undermine the nascent state he was trying to build, he sought to avoid any military undertaking that was not required to defend Turkey's most vital interests. He counseled in particular against engagement in the conflict-prone Middle East, where European powers were establishing their own competing spheres of influence.

Moreover, Atatürk instinctively looked beyond Turkey's borders. He saw the Middle East as having fallen behind the West in terms of technology and general development. He viewed Islam in the Middle East as frozen in time, dominated by suspicion of the West and equal rights for women, and emphasizing the authority of Muslim clerics over individual rights and rational thinking. Atatürk sought to insulate Turkey from what he viewed as a Middle Eastern mindset of stagnation and to propel the republic toward modernization. His foreign policy thus focused on moving a proud Turkey closer to Europe, in keeping with 14 centuries of Turkic migration from East to West.

From Atatürk to the AKP

After Atatürk's death, his successors followed his admonition to avoid conflict with countries that could threaten the nascent Turkish Republic. Although Turkey stayed out of World War II, the end of that global conflict brought a new danger, which compelled the country to break out of isolationism and seek new allies. During the war, an expansionist Soviet Union, on Turkey's eastern border, took over former Ottoman territories in the Balkans. Ankara was alarmed by the possibility of Moscow attempting to satisfy its longstanding quest for an outlet to the Mediterranean and control of the Turkish Straits.

Seeking partners to contain Soviet expansion, Turkey joined the UN coalition led by the United States to counter Moscow's ambitions on the Korean peninsula. Korea was worlds away, but Turkey's leaders saw their involvement in that conflict as the price necessary for inclusion in the Pax Americana. As Ankara deepened its military cooperation with Washington, the leader of the Euro-Atlantic community, it grew comfortable with NATO and joined that alliance in 1952. For the following four decades, Turkey secured NATO's southern flank against the Soviet Union, while pursuing peace at home and peace in the world through collaboration with its new Euro-Atlantic allies.

NATO membership created the strategic opening for Turkey to seek closer relations with the European Community. In 1959, Ankara requested an association agreement with the EC. Delayed by a military coup, Turkey finally concluded the pact, known as the Ankara Agreement, in 1963. That development launched an extended period of Turkey's adaptation toward EC norms, after which Turkey would apply for EC membership. At first, Turkey remained hesitant to surrender its sovereignty to a multilateral organization. (Ankara's efforts to adapt its norms to EC standards came to a full stop after the 1980 military coup.)

Ankara eventually applied for EC membership in 1987. Still, most Turks retained a strong nationalist pride and a skeptical view of reform "demands"; they were viewed as dictates of EC bureaucrats, even if all realists understood that Turkey would have to play by European rules if it joined this exclusive European club.

Part of the resistance to EC-mandated change stemmed from their traumatic experience with Europe during the long twilight of the Ottoman Empire. Turks still smarted at European powers referring to the Ottoman Empire as "the sick man of Europe" during the late nineteenth century and humiliating Turkey with the Treaty of Sèvres in 1920. Moreover, Turks viewed Europeans as insensitive and naïve for failing to appreciate the strategic significance of their republic as the only secular democracy with a Muslim majority population in the Middle East (and Europe) and as a bulwark against Soviet expansion. By the 1970s, while Turks embraced modernization through Europeanization, they also felt compelled to rely on themselves at times to defend their nation and its secular democracy.

The Turkish Republic did its best to bid farewell to empire. But Turkish leaders were not willing to abandon all memories of an imperial past or all responsibility for Turks living abroad.

In 1974, Turkey sent military forces to Cyprus. The declared mission: to protect the Turkish Cypriot minority during intercommunal clashes following a coup inspired by Greece's junta that toppled the democratically elected government of Archbishop Makarios. Europeans denounced that military operation as an invasion of a sovereign country, bringing the Turkish bid for a place in Europe to a halt. Ankara viewed that criticism from Europe as a price it had to pay for fulfilling what it regarded as its responsibility as a guarantor of Turkish Cypriot security under the Treaties of Guarantee, which it had concluded with Greece and the United Kingdom in 1960.

The Cyprus crisis also damaged Ankara's relations with the United States, but Ankara and Washington remained close NATO allies. This partnership was strengthened in the 1980s, when Prime Minister and President Turgut Özal liberalized Turkey economically and politically, and especially when Turkey supported the United States (albeit belatedly) in the Persian Gulf War of 1990. Many Kemalists, including those on the general staff, opposed Özal's backing of the U.S. invasion of Iraq as a violation of Atatürk's admonition against enmeshing Turkey in conflicts in the Middle East. Özal countered that it was time for a bold Turkish foreign policy that moved beyond a status quo vision. The wily and shrewd Özal said that it was better for Turkey to have a seat at the table than be on the menu. By siding with the United States, Turkey could secure economic and strategic benefits following the inevitable U.S. victory, which would greatly outweigh the advantages of continued isolationism.

Turkey's support for U.S. efforts during the Persian Gulf War laid the foundation for a strategic partnership between Ankara and Washington. Though many Turks were disappointed that they did not receive even more benefits from such support, top Turkish government officials were grateful for Washington's goodwill. And the United States tried to compensate Turkey for economic hardship resulting from the U.S.-led embargo of Iraq, Turkey's southern neighbor and primary oil supplier. Washington led the charge at the International Monetary Fund in securing massive loans to keep the Turkish economy afloat.

Washington also helped Ankara elevate its strategic importance by emphasizing Turkey's role as the strategic connection between Europe and the former Soviet states of Central Asia/ the Caucasus. This vision of a new Silk Road evolved into a shared Turkish-American effort to develop an east-west corridor to deliver Caspian oil and gas to European and global markets. The two nations expanded their partnership to include Azerbaijan and Georgia, culminating in two of the world's most complex and strategically significant energy pipelines, the Baku-Tbilisi-Ceyhan oil and South Caucasus gas lines.

This vision of a more strategically relevant Turkey appealed to the Kemalists, who were eager to reconnect with their Turkic kin to the east. Some Islamists, like the Gülenists, also sought a foreign policy shift toward the east, which would enable them to revive common Islamic roots with Turkic countries. The United States welcomed Turkey's readiness to help bolster the sovereignty, independence, and prosperity of these new countries, while diversifying global energy supplies.

Tensions nevertheless remained in bilateral relations. A central issue was the U.S. request for Turkish support in defending Iraq's Kurdish population following the 1991 Persian Gulf War. Kemalists feared that by protecting Iraqi Kurds near the Turkey-Iraq border, Ankara might aggravate separatist tensions that could spill into Turkey's Kurdish community, which sought autonomy and/or independence. Those concerns rekindled historic Kemalist suspicions that the Euro-Atlantic community might support the Kurds' quest for an autonomous entity in southeastern Turkey. They recalled how European powers used U.S. President Woodrow Wilson's call for self-determination at the end of World War I to demand an independent Kurdistan in the Treaty of Sèvres, which was forced on a feeble Ottoman government.

Despite such concerns, Ankara granted Washington's request to allow American planes to patrol and enforce a no-fly zone in northern Iraq from İncirlik Airbase near Adana in south central Turkey. Washington worked to assuage Ankara's fear of Kurdish separatism by cooperating on counterterrorism, especially by providing crucial support in capturing Abdullah Öcalan, the leader of the terrorist Kurdish Workers' Party (PKK) hiding in Kenya in 1999.

The ability of Washington and Ankara to manage historical fears and foster operational cooperation on these complex and sensitive security issues generated a new and positive mood in bilateral relations. That in turn enabled Turkish leaders to think more broadly about security partnership. In the late 1990s, Turkey expanded this developing pattern of cooperation to include the United States' closest ally in the Middle

East, Israel. As the only other democracy in the Middle East, Israel's secular government and European orientation made it a logical partner for Ankara, despite anti-Israeli sentiment among Muslims in other countries.

For several decades, Ankara had tempered its response to international crises involving Israel. Turkey had been one of the first countries to recognize Israel (in 1949) and had not supported the Arabs in either the 1967 or the 1973 wars. In the 1980s and 1990s, Turkey and Israel recognized their shared interests in protecting their secular democratic systems against Iran's Islamism and Syria's support for the PKK and anti-Israel terrorists. Together with the United States, the two counties developed an informal partnership to counter the Iranian and Syrian threats, as Ankara strove to ensure Atatürk's goal of peace at home and peace in the world.

New Foreign Policy Trends in the 1990s

While successive Turkish governments were strengthening cooperation with the United States and Israel into strategic partnerships in defense of Euro-Atlantic solidarity and secular democracy, Turkey's Islamist leaders were moving in a different direction. The Islamists sought to revive a pan-Islamic identity in which Turks would be part of a global Islamic community. During his brief period of rule in 1996–97, Prime Minister Necmettin Erbakan sought alliances, and a place for Turkey, in the Islamic world. Islamist political strategists believed globalization would generate backlash; nations would protect their identities by embracing their local cultures, which for Turkish Islamists would mean restoring Islam as a key determinant of the Turkish identity, with *sharia* as a core principle of governance. They argued that Turkey could become a major power by restoring its connections with Muslim countries of the post-Ottoman "space."

Reacting to this Islamist push, many nationalists and mainstream Kemalists pressed Ankara to reorient its foreign policy around Turkey's historical ties to its Turkic brethren to the east. The collapse of the Soviet Union had created new opportunities for Turkish political, military, and business leaders to revive pan-Turkism in Azerbaijan and Central Asia. In addition, in the mid-1990s, Turkish President Süleyman Demirel collaborated with his Georgian and Azerbaijani counterparts, Eduard Shevardnadze and Heydar Aliyev, respectively, in calling for restoration of the fabled Great Silk Road, which had linked Asia and Europe via trade routes stretching across the Caspian Sea and South Caucasus into Turkey. As noted above, the United States embraced this vision, and President Bill Clinton joined the three regional presidents in pursuing the east-west energy corridor consisting of the Baku-Tbilisi-Ceyhan oil and South Caucasus gas pipelines.

During the late '90s, a third foreign policy trend, known as Eurasianism, emerged in narrow Kemalist circles in response to both the Turkish government's embrace of the United States and the Islamists' strong preference for closer relations with fellow Muslims. The Eurasianists held that Turkey's national interests were no longer served by acting as the West's junior partner. Instead, Turkey should form a strategic alliance with Eurasian powers Russia and Iran, which had threatened Turkey's vital interests in previous centuries but with whom Ankara could now work to foster a new era of economic growth and regional stability. Perhaps surprisingly, some of the key proponents of the Eurasianist vision, which ran counter to Atatürk's call for Turkey to keep aligning itself with the West, were senior Turkish military officers. They chafed at the Europeans having invited former Ottoman dependencies and Warsaw Pact adversaries (such as Romania and Bulgaria) to join the EU ahead of NATO ally Turkey.

All three alternative foreign policy visions were nationalist at their core, sharing a sense of frustration that the West had not helped Turkey realize its full strategic potential. The adherents of these visions shared the concern that Turkey was still perceived as the sick man of Europe and insisted that Turkey assert itself to remind the world it was too strategically important to be ignored. This combination of insecurity and pride led the Islamists and Eurasianists to distrust the Euro-Atlantic community. The pan-Turkists welcomed cooperation with the United States to elevate Turkey's strategic impact on the South Caucasus and Central Asia. But they shared the ambition of the Islamists and Eurasianists to nudge Turkish foreign policy in new directions. Members of all three schools sought to move Turkey away from passive partnership with the Euro-Atlantic community and from a position on the periphery of the West, toward active assertion of the nation's role as a regional power.

AKP Foreign-Policy Reorientation

Those contending views of strategy provided the context for the AKP to develop its own foreign policy following its November 2002 electoral victory. The party's key foreign policy theorist was Ahmet Davutoğlu, a brilliant professor who became chief foreign policy advisor to Prime Minister Erdoğan and then foreign minister. Davutoğlu laid out the fundamentals of his thinking in his influential book, *Strategic Depth: Turkey's International Position* (2001). This philosophical and political treatise recognized that the end of the Cold War had generated new challenges and fresh opportunities for Turkey to elevate its strategic significance as a major regional power.[2] Rather than limiting its role to serving as a "wing" of the Euro-Atlantic community, Davutoğlu argued, Turkey should enhance its strategic value to the West and the world by adding to its foreign policy agenda such new tasks as mediating conflicts in the Middle East and Afghanistan, and expanding Turkey's diplomatic and commercial opportunities in Africa and Latin America.

At the core of Davutoğlu's vision was the quest for Turkey to have "zero problems with its neighbors." By resolving all serious disputes with neighboring countries, Turkey could become a regional locomotive of peace and prosperity, thereby serving the fundamental interests of its Euro-Atlantic allies and remaining consistent with Atatürk's fundamental foreign policy tenet.

Critics label Davutoğlu's approach "Neo-Ottomanism," suggesting a combination of imperiousness and Islamism that shifts the primary axis of Turkish foreign policy from an east-west vector (extending from Turkey through NATO/EU to the United States) to a north-south axis (stretching from Russia to Iran and Turkey's other Muslim neighbors). Davutoğlu rejects these characterizations. He notes that Turkey is engaging with surrounding countries not out of post-imperial nostalgia but due to inescapable factors of geography and history, which dictate a range of connections between Turkey and the successor states of the Ottoman Empire. He calls for Turkey to rely on its "soft power" of diplomacy and economic engagement to take advantage of these manifold cultural and historical links to foster regional stability and economic integration. In response to accusations that Ankara is using its soft power to foster pan-Islamist solidarity, Davutoğlu notes that only four of Turkey's twelve neighbors have Muslim-majority populations, and that Ankara is deepening its engagement with NATO and the EU as it resolves bilateral problems with Syria and Iran.

The AKP and the Middle East: Realpolitik and Islamism

The debate outlined above is playing out with particular vigor in the Middle East. The AKP's critics argue that Ankara's current foreign policy departs from decades of adherence to Atatürk's admonition to avoid entanglements in the Middle East, except in rare instances when Turkey's vital national interests are at stake. During the 1990s, Turkey's one key relationship in the Middle East was a strategic partnership with Israel.

Under the AKP, however, the Turkish government has reversed this strategy, seeking deeper engagement with Arab states and distancing itself from Israel. Rather than sustaining a strategic partnership, Ankara now treats Israel as a subject for mediation efforts on a par with Arab states. Since 2004, Turkey has thus sought to expand its ties with Syria and mediate the Syria-Israel conflict, even when the Euro-Atlantic community and Israel pressed for isolation of the Asad regime. During 2007–08, Turkey hosted five rounds of indirect talks between Syria and Israel but suspended this effort after harshly criticizing Israel's military operations in Gaza (see below). In 2006, Turkey sent peacekeeping forces to Lebanon following the brief war between Israel and Hezbollah; since then, it has tried to foster reconciliation among Lebanon's fractious political groupings, while criticizing Israel for its military operation into Lebanon. The AKP government has offered to mediate the Israel-Palestinian conflict, even while focusing its efforts on providing financial and technical assistance to Palestinian authorities (primarily Hamas in Gaza) and sharply criticizing Israel.

The Turkish government contends that such efforts reflect not an ideological push to replace Israel with Muslim-majority Middle Eastern states as key partners but a desire to foster regional peace and economic integration. Foreign Minister Davutoğlu often argues with conviction that because the share of Turkey's total trade volume accounted for by commerce with neighboring Syria, Iran, and Iraq increased during the period of 2003 to 2009 from 8 percent to 32 percent, the Turkish economy weathered the 2008–09 global economic downturn with less damage relative to other major economies. But Turkey's sharp political attacks on Israel starting 2009 suggest that other factors were involved.

Israel's military operation in Gaza in late 2008 shook the Turkish government, which was hosting indirect talks between Israel and Syria that seemed on the verge of a breakthrough. The AKP government was thus upset at the timing of the Israeli operation and repulsed by what it characterized as "inhumane" attacks on Palestinian civilians. The harshness of Turkey's criticism of Israel was unprecedented. It exploded on the world stage at the 2009 World Economic Forum cited above. During a panel discussion, while Israeli President Peres tried to explain the Gaza incursion from Israel's perspective, Prime Minister Erdoğan accused Israel of transforming Gaza into an "open-air prison" and said, "I know very well how you hit and killed children on beaches." Erdoğan then stormed off the stage in anger, stunning President Peres, the audience in Davos, and many in the international community. When a journalist asked about Peres' reply to her husband's accusations, Emine Erdoğan said tearfully, "All of it was lies."[3]

In the immediate aftermath of that confrontation, the AKP pursued an anti-Israel course. Upon returning to Istanbul airport, Prime Minister Erdoğan was greeted by a cheering throng of approximately 5,000 early in the morning. The emotionally charged demonstrators carried Turkish and Hamas flags and signs proclaiming "Erdoğan, the new Saladdin" (referring to the Muslim leader who recaptured Jerusalem from the Crusaders in 1187), "Erdoğan, our Conqueror" (referring to

Mehmet II, who conquered Constantinople in 1453), and "Erdoğan, a new world leader." The prime minister suggested that Israel be ousted from the United Nations and called on the UN to condemn Israeli "war crimes" in Gaza.

Internationally, reaction among non-Arabs to Erdoğan's outburst in Davos ranged from disappointment to shock. In the United States, the American Jewish Committee, for years a strong supporter of Turkey, declared the attack on President Peres and Israel "a public disgrace" and "gasoline on the fire of surging anti-Semitism." Academics and civil-society activists in Washington and many parts of Europe lamented that Erdoğan's anti-Israel vitriol would make it impossible for Turkey to help mediate the Middle East peace process. In October 2009, Turkey refused to invite Israel to a joint military exercise that also included the United States and Italy, an event that had occurred annually since the mid-1990s, citing lingering anger over Israel's raid into Gaza in 2008. After the United States and Italy withdrew from the exercise in protest, a high-ranking Israeli government official told the Israeli daily *Ma'ariv* that Israel and other Western countries were concerned that Erdoğan was leading Turkey through a gradual "process of Islamization." Added the official, "Until today, Turkey has been the antithesis of Iran—a secular Muslim country with a tolerant constitution, which would like to become a member of the European Union."

Many observers note that the drift toward Islamization is also evident in AKP's approach to the Palestinian authorities. They argue that if Ankara's sole aim was to improve relations with its neighbors (and near neighbors), it would seek close relations with both secular President Mahmoud Abbas in Ramallah and Islamist Hamas leaders in Gaza. Instead, the Turkish government has broken with Abbas, whom Erdoğan disparaged as the "head of an illegitimate government," and called on the world to "recognize Hamas as the legitimate government of the Palestinian people." Turkey's AKP government was also the first to extend an official invitation to Khaled Meshal, the Syrian-based leader of Hamas's militant wing, whom the West condemns as a terrorist leader. That action marked a sharp departure with previous Turkish governments, which considered Hamas a terrorist and Islamist organization that threatened the existence of Israel and secular governments in general.

A particularly stark example of this apparent shift toward pan-Islamism in the AKP's foreign policy is Turkey's budding relationship with Sudan. The government chose Sudan, a veritable pariah in the international order of states, as a key ally on the continent. Prime Minister Erdoğan broke with his European and American allies over Sudan during his 2006 visit to that country, when he proclaimed that no genocide had occurred there. The government twice welcomed Sudanese President al-Bashir to Turkey in 2008. Then, the following January, the day after his attack in Davos on Israel for "killing innocent civilians," Erdoğan invited the Sudanese vice president Ali Osman Taha to visit Ankara. All that occurred in the face of near-universal condemnation (including by the International Criminal Court) of Sudan's genocidal campaign against its own citizens. The prime minister responded to criticism of his embrace of Sudan's leaders by claiming in November 2009 that "a Muslim cannot commit genocide."

The AKP's efforts to improve Turkey's relations with Saudi Arabia also seem to indicate a pan-Islamist shift in foreign policy. Previous Turkish governments had usually held the Saudi regime at arm's length, fearing an invasion by the country's Wahhabi interpretation of Islam, which seeks to replace secular democracies around the globe with *sharia* rule. Although Turgut Özal briefly cultivated Saudi détente during his presidency, the Kemalist military and civilian establishments scuttled his efforts, and subsequent Turkish governments did not restart them. But in 2006, Erdoğan invited King Abdullah to make the first visit to Turkey by a Saudi king in 40 years. During his third visit, two years later, Erdoğan and President Gül took the unprecedented step of visiting the king at his hotel, rather than receiving him in a governmental office in accordance with universal diplomatic practice.

An analogous shift—of longer standing—also seems evident in the AKP government's approach to Iran, which, like Sudan, has a radical Islamist regime. Nearly all previous Turkish governments had kept their distance from Tehran, as they did from Riyadh, fearing the potential spread of Islamist thinking to Turkey. But Erbakan and his fellow Islamists welcomed the Iranian Revolution in 1979. Three decades later, an AKP government made Turkey the first NATO country to host a visit by Mahmud Ahmadinejad. Erdoğan refers to Ahmadinejad by affectionate title "*değerli kardeşim*," which means "my dear brother." AKP leaders make a spirited defense of their outreach to Iran, citing the two countries' stable border since 1639, growing economic ties, and common fight against PKK terrorists.

Despite their declared opposition to nuclear weapons in principle, the AKP leaders, and Erdoğan in particular, further argue that Iran's pursuit of peaceful nuclear technologies is justified, given Israel's assumed possession of nuclear weapons. The AKP consistently avoids answering questions about whether it believes that Tehran is trying to develop them. Turkey has stood apart from the United States, and even Russia and China, in refusing to condemn Iran's nuclear enrichment program at the UN's International Atomic Energy Agency in November 2009. This dissembling with regard to Iran, coupled with harsh attacks on Israel, marks such a profound departure from Turkey's previous policies that something beyond realpolitik must be an important factor. Many observers increasingly believe this additional factor to be a pan-Islamist vision shared by the Turkish and Iranian governments.

Turkey-EU Relations: Commitment or Deception?

The AKP's Kemalist opponents also warn that an Islamist tint is coloring Turkey's relations with its European allies. One stark indicator was Ankara's opposition to the candidacy of Danish Prime Minister Anders Fogh Rasmussen as NATO Secretary General in 2009. The Turkish government protested that a Danish secretary general would alienate the world's Muslims, some of whom, in 2006, reacted angrily to satirical images of the Prophet Muhammad published in Danish news-papers. Another indicator, that same year, was Turkey's deci-sion to join Spain as co-chair of the UN's Alliance of Civilizations, which aims to foster dialogue and cooperation between the West and the Islamic world. Kemalist critics ar-gued the AKP was positioning Turkey as the representative of the "Muslim world" and a counterpart *to* the West, rather than as a member *of* the West. Senior AKP members strength-ened that perception through frequent attacks on Western Europe as "Islamophobic," and Erdoğan's designation of the West as "immoral."[4] Ankara further distanced itself from its Euro-Atlantic allies in the wake of the Russia-Georgia war in August 2008, when it launched its Caucasus Peace and Stabil-ity Platform with Russia, Georgia, Armenia, and Azerbaijan, but without the United States and the EU.

Senior AKP leaders argue that they are simply adding fresh initiatives to a foreign policy agenda that reflects both new post-Cold War opportunities and continuing commitment to Euro-Atlantic engagement. Party leaders stress that they are deepening Turkey's engagement in Afghanistan—through the training of Afghan military and police, financial assistance, and a provincial reconstruction team, as well as a third term com-manding the International Security Assistance Force in that country. They further argue that they have done more to ad-vance Turkey's EU candidacy during seven years in power than other governments have done during the previous 40 years. (AKP leaders attribute a sharp decrease in the EU's approval rating among Turks to European leaders treating Turkey's candidacy unfairly; many Turks cite in particular the preference of French President Nicolas Sarkozy and German Chancellor Angela Merkel for Turkey to have no more than "privileged [rather than full] partnership.")

In addition, Turks have grown disillusioned with the EU over the Cyprus problem. In 2003, at the height of its effort to convince the EU to begin accession talks with Turkey, the AKP broke with four decades of national policy and withdrew support from Turkish Cypriot leader Rauf Denktaş. His stubbornness and determination in supporting Turkish Cypriots' political rights and a Turkish identity on the island won him strong popularity among Kemalists in Turkey. But Western leaders viewed Denktaş as obstructive and unreasonable. After the AKP government abandoned him, he was replaced as "president" following the election in 2004 of the more moderate Mehmet Ali Talat.

The AKP government then pressed Turkish Cypriots to accept the Cyprus settlement plan drafted by then-UN Secretary General Kofi Annan. In a landmark referendum in April 2004, they approved the Annan plan, but Greek Cypriots rejected it. The AKP won considerable support from the EU and the United States for taking these bold and constructive steps on Cyprus. The EU dealt itself another black eye, in the view of Turks across the political spectrum, by subsequently failing to fulfill its pledge to enhance trade ties with the Turkish Cypriot community.

Popular support for the EU in Turkey plummeted from its high of 70 percent in 2002. In 2007, according to a survey by the German Marshall Fund, it stood at 32 percent. In addition, the survey showed that only 34 percent of Turks reported feeling that they share common values with the West, and that 55 percent of Turks (and 57 percent of Europeans) believed that Turkey as a nation does not share the core values of Europe or the Western tradition.

It is perhaps impossible to discern whether this sharp decline in Turkish support for the EU results more from the rhetoric and policies of European leaders or from those of the AKP. Many Kemalists believe that the AKP has followed a tactical and cynical approach to EU accession. In their view, the party initially consolidated its domestic and international support by offering reassurance that Turkey would remain committed to EU accession, but later used the EU accession process to restore Islam as the prime determinant of Turkish identity.

Immediately after its 2002 electoral victory, the AKP's critics say, the party started working on a package of constitutional reforms to fulfill EU criteria for beginning accession talks. Senior AKP leaders regularly visited Brussels and other European capitals to make Turkey's case. When, in October 2005, the EU finally began accession talks with Turkey, the AKP seemed legitimized as a pro-Western political party pursuing Turkey's traditional foreign policy, and support for the EU among pro-Western liberal Turks increased significantly. After October 2005, however, the Turkish parliament seemed to slow progress on EU-mandated reforms and instead pursued legal changes that would advance an Islamist social agenda, such as allowing female students to wear the Islamic headscarf in universities. Erdoğan disclosed his priorities in his remarkable statement in Berlin in 2008, when he urged

Germany's large Turkish population to resist assimilation into mainstream German society, calling assimilation a "crime against humanity."[5] If Turkey were to enter the European society of nations, the AKP seemed determined that it enter it as a Muslim nation.

U.S.-Turkish Relations: Breakdown . . .

Turkey's waning enthusiasm for the EU between 2003 and 2005 coincided with a dramatic deterioration in its relationship with its most important ally, the United States. While the governments of both countries subsequently worked hard to restore a sense of dependable cooperation, the U.S.-Turkish partnership has yet to regain the level it enjoyed in the late 1990s.

Washington's confidence in its strong relationship with Ankara was shattered on March 1, 2003, when the Turkish parliament voted to reject the United States' request to transport troops and military equipment across Turkey and into Iraq. The vote occurred after months of negotiations over economic, political, and military agreements plus an $8 billion U.S.-assistance program (which could have grown into more than $20 billion in loan guarantees). The unusual nature of the vote prompted suspicions in Washington that the AKP had found a clever way to reject the U.S. request without appearing to do so intentionally. Initially, parliament voted to approve the U.S. request, but then nullified the action on procedural grounds (the presence of too many non-voting deputies on the floor denied a quorum by three votes).

Rather than managing AKP's parliamentary faction to ensure a positive vote, Prime Minister Erdoğan simply asked his party's deputies to vote "with their conscience." Top Washington officials were disappointed with what appeared to be a lack of AKP commitment to secure a positive outcome for perhaps the most important vote in the history of American-Turkish relations. U.S. Defense Department officials were also upset with the Kemalists, especially the military. Deputy Secretary of Defense Paul Wolfowitz lamented at the time that the Turkish military "did not play the strong leadership role . . . that we would have expected."[6]

Despite their deep disappointment with that vote, senior U.S. officials tried to avoid a breakdown in American-Turkish relations on the eve of the war in Iraq. Although it was at that juncture impossible to proceed with the original U.S. deal, Washington did offer Ankara a $1 billion grant to help sustain international confidence in the Turkish banking system and economy should the upcoming war threaten to destabilize the Turkish economy. Congress required only that to receive the grant, Turkey must maintain its IMF-agreed reform program (to promote the confidence mentioned above) and refrain from unilateral military action in northern Iraq.

Turkish leaders across the political spectrum reacted negatively to this U.S. assistance offer, misinterpreting it as an attempt by the United States to dictate economic and military policy to their government. In hindsight, the AKP appears to have opposed the war in principle; Davutoğlu, then the top foreign affairs advisor to the prime minister, joined other AKP leaders in warning against Turkey being seen as a war-maker by granting the U.S. request. Many parliamentarians believed that their "no" vote would stop the war—the United States would be unable to attack Iraq without Turkey's support—and Turkey would emerge as a major regional power that had secured peace.

Elements of the Turkish military also opposed the war. They worried that the United States had no plan for post-war Iraq. They feared that after Saddam Hussein's dictatorial rule, a power vacuum would emerge, and Iraq's various ethnic and sectarian groups could pull the country apart. That could lead to an Iraqi Kurdish push for autonomy, which could spill into Turkey, where the army had been at war for over a decade with Kurdish separatists and PKK terrorists at a cost of over 40,000 Turkish lives. Such fears were aggravated by talk in U.S. academic and political circles of possible autonomy for Iraq's Kurdish region, echoing historical recollections of the 1920 Treaty of Sèvres, when European powers forced the Ottoman authorities to accept an autonomous Kurdish region as they schemed to divide Turkish lands among themselves. President Bush attempted to counter these fears by pledging to Prime Minister Erdoğan that the United States would help eliminate the threat posed by PKK terrorists based in northern Iraq and operating in Turkey.

Following the fall of Saddam Hussein, as weeks and months passed with no U.S. military action against PKK terrorists in northern Iraq, Turkish military commanders grew frustrated with the United States. These tensions exacerbated suspicions among many Turkish officers that Washington had helped engineer the AKP's electoral victory in 2002. Fueling that suspicion was the fact that Bush had hosted Recep Tayyip Erdoğan in the White House in December 2002, before he had been elected to parliament and while he was still banned from politics for his conviction of subversion.

Meanwhile, the U.S. military was losing faith in their Turkish counterparts. Many U.S. officers blamed Turkey for increased U.S. casualties resulting from parliament's decision to deny the United States the "Northern Option" that would have allowed an attack against Iraq from both north and south. They worried that the Turkish military was contemplating unilateral operations against the PKK in northern Iraq. U.S. commanders also grew annoyed with Ankara's urging Washington to divert troops from the main fight against Saddam Hussein's supporters to the North. And they further worried that the Turkish Special Forces were fomenting political unrest between Ankara's Turkoman clients and the Kurdish population of northern Iraq, especially in the volatile city of Kirkuk.

Amid these tensions, on July 4, 2003, American soldiers arrested, and placed hoods over the heads of, eleven Turkish Special Forces officers in the Iraqi city of Sulaymaniyah. U.S. military officials were outraged by the presence of these crack Turkish troops, out of uniform and in a politically volatile area of northern Iraq. U.S. military leaders accused the captured Turkish soldiers of plotting to assassinate local Kurdish officials, which could have generated a wave of political instability and violence in the one region of Iraq that was relatively stable.

Turkish soldiers and private citizens, for their part, were enraged that their proud Special Forces officers were humiliated by their key NATO ally and treated like terrorists. For many in the lower ranks of the Turkish military, that amounted to an unforgivable insult by the United States, and it heightened anti-American sentiments in Turkish society at large. Most Turks did not notice when, months later, several Turkish Special Forces commanders were disciplined and/or demoted for their responsibility in the Sulaymaniyah incident. The damage had been done: distrust had increased significantly among important segments of the population in both countries.

Turkey's general public now began to blame the United States for renewed terrorism and ethnic tension emanating from Turkey's Kurdish population. A wave of anti-Americanism swept across popular culture. The novel *Metal Storm* became a runaway bestseller with a plot that featured the United States launching a war against Turkey, and Turkey being saved by a Special Forces soldier who detonates a nuclear weapon and vaporizes Washington, D.C. At around the same time, the film *Valley of the Wolves: Iraq* became a blockbuster, with its portrayal of U.S. troops in Iraq as bloodthirsty Christian fundamentalists who enjoy slaughtering innocent Iraqis. The film includes graphic and incendiary dramatizations of the Sulaymaniyah incident, Abu Ghraib prison, and a fictional American Jewish doctor harvesting human organs. *Valley of the Wolves* was the largest-budget film produced in Turkey to date, and was accepted by tens of millions of Turks as a truthful portrayal of their American ally.

Rather than correcting these incendiary mischaracterizations of the United States, prominent AKP figures fanned growing anti-Americanism. Speaker of Parliament Bülent Arınç praised *Valley of the Wolves* as "a great film that will go down in history." When asked by the state-owned Anatolia News Agency whether he believed the movie reflected reality, he replied with an astounding "yes, exactly." Prime Minister Erdoğan's wife, Emine, proclaimed that she felt "proud" watching the film. In April 2004, Mehmet Elkatmış, chairman of parliament's human rights commission, accused the United States of "committing genocide and a violent crime against humanity" during its siege of Falluja, Iraq. "Neither the Pharaohs, nor Hitler and Mussolini, had committed such crimes," Elkatmış added. He further suggested that the United States might have deployed nuclear weapons in Iraq, while Prime Minister Erdoğan opined that weapons of mass destruction might have been used in Falluja.

As with AKP's harsh attacks on Israel (and the subsidized publication of *Mein Kampf* and *The Protocols of the Elders of Zion* at this same time), the vitriol of the above statements by senior AKP leaders seemed to prove an agenda derived from considerations far beyond those of realpolitik. After all, if Turkish leaders worried about destabilization spilling from Iraq into Turkey, it made little sense to stoke popular anger against the country that was leading an international coalition in Iraq. Many observers, even Kemalists who felt frustrated by the U.S. decision to launch the war in Iraq over Turkey's objection, surmised that the AKP was exploiting anti-American sentiment to appeal to fellow Muslims and Islamists and advance the party's larger agenda.

Gradually, the AKP government softened its rhetoric, realizing that the political costs of estranging its most important ally outweighed the ideological benefits of appealing to the world's Islamists. The United States had been trying to repair relations with Turkey since 2004, when it pressed successfully for a NATO summit to be held in Istanbul that June.

. . . and Rebuilding

Prime Minister Erdoğan's visit to Washington a year later marked a turning point on Turkey's part. Following his meeting in the Oval Office with President Bush, Erdoğan began to issue statements referring to the United States as Turkey's friend and partner. Such statements helped build diplomatic momentum, as U.S. and Turkish diplomats worked together to assemble a common set of shared interests to repair the bilateral partnership. Their efforts culminated in July 2006 with the signing of the "Shared Vision Document," which outlined ten core areas for cooperation and regularized joint efforts by forming bilateral working groups.

A true breakthrough between Washington and Ankara occurred when Bush and Erdoğan met in November 2007. Immediately following that discussion, Bush announced in the Oval Office, with Erdoğan at his side, that the United States considered the PKK an enemy of Turkey and therefore of the United States, and that the two leaders had agreed on a new intelligence-sharing mechanism to facilitate joint efforts to defeat the terrorist group.[7] Official relations between the two governments steadily improved, with Ankara finally satisfied that the United States was fulfilling Bush's pledge of four and a half years earlier to prevent northern Iraq from remaining a sanctuary for the PKK.

Nonetheless, popular anti-Americanism remained strong in Turkey. People across Turkey's political spectrum blamed President Bush's foreign policy for the decline in U.S. popularity. They anticipated that a new U.S. president would bring a return of traditionally positive Turkish attitudes toward the United States. Indeed, most Turks cheered the 2008 election of Barack Obama, believing that an American president with a Muslim heritage would be able to appreciate issues relevant to the "Muslim world." A president with the middle name Hussein stood in stark contrast to the evangelical Christian George W. Bush, who many Turks believed had embarked upon a twenty-first-century "Crusade" after the September 11 terror attacks. Residents of a remote village in Turkey even sacrificed forty-four sheep to celebrate President Obama's election as the forty-fourth President.

In April 2009, Obama made Turkey the first stop on his initial overseas trip, which also included several European destinations. The U.S. president was making a conscious effort to restore a sense of partnership in American-Turkish relations—and subtly underscoring U.S. support for Turkey's EU aspirations. (This was, after all, an explicitly *European* trip.) He delivered to the Turkish parliament a thoughtful speech that demonstrated an understanding of Turkey's strategic potential as a key partner for the Euro-Atlantic community and as a secular democracy with a Muslim majority population.

The visit won the new president a measure of popular acclaim in Turkey, with many analysts claiming that bilateral relations were back to normal. In Istanbul, he helped broker a historic agreement between Turkey and Armenia to normalize their relations, reopen and recognize their border, and examine their sometimes tragic and painful history (especially the mass killings and forced exile of over one million Armenians by Ottoman troops in 1915). Following the Obama visit, the United States embraced the AKP's expressed desire to improve relations with its neighbors, especially in the Middle East, and help mediate conflicts there, while also collaborating on issues involving Afghanistan and Pakistan.

Yet despite the success of Obama's trip to Turkey and his administration's effort to bolster American-Turkish relations, the United States remained more unpopular in Turkey than in any other country in the world. As mentioned earlier, a Pew poll in summer 2009 found that favorability toward the United States had risen in Turkey by only two percentage points following the presidential visit.

That statistic greatly surprised many U.S. and European observers. It appeared that the United States' unpopularity in Turkey could not be dismissed as "anti-Bushism" but reflected instead a deeper form of anti-Americanism that had emerged since the AKP came to power in late 2002. Clearly, U.S. military actions in Iraq and a conviction that the Bush administration was pursuing a global "war against Islam" catalyzed popular sentiment. Yet the unprecedented depth of the sentiment remained surprising: 71 percent of Turks considering their strategic partner of 2001 a "potential military threat" in June 2003. That suggested that Turkey's political leaders had stoked anti-U.S. sentiment.

In its relations with Washington, as with Israel, the Palestinian authorities, Sudan, and Iran, the AKP government seemed driven at least in part by a pan-Islamist agenda. At times, it required the AKP to depict the United States as less an ally than an adversary. The Obama diplomacy could neither change that tactic nor drain Turkish political swamps of anti-Americanism; that sentiment, in Turkey as in other Muslim lands, had assumed a force of its own, beyond reason and rational analysis.

At the same time, the AKP government has also demonstrated a growing understanding that it cannot completely ignore the forces of realpolitik. Perhaps no Turkish government, regardless of its ideology, can escape Ankara's enduring commitment to sustain a Turkish Cypriot community on Cyprus or to work in partnership wherever possible with the United States. Political reality also drives Ankara's growing cooperation with Russia, which emerged in 2008 as Turkey's largest trading partner (and supplier of nearly two-thirds of its natural gas).

Turkish foreign policy is undeniably in a state of flux. A mix of Islamist ideology and realpolitik has redirected Ankara away from its reliance on NATO and the United States as the foundation of national security. Today, Turkey is renewing its aspiration to emerge as an indispensable leader in the vast region stretching from the Balkans to the Altai Mountains and the Persian Gulf. Such ambition, reflected in the AKP's slogan of "Zero problems with Turkey's neighbors," faces inherent contradictions. Azerbaijan, traditionally one of Turkey's closest allies, is furious with the latter's effort to normalize relations with Armenia in the absence of a settlement to the Nagorno-Karabakh conflict that fuels Azerbaijan's long-running feud with Armenia. Troubled relations with Baku complicate Turkey's quest to elevate its strategic importance to the EU as the key transit state for diversified flows of natural gas to Europe from Azerbaijan.

Despite those contradictory elements, Ankara's quest to advance peace and prosperity in many of its neighboring countries reflects key objectives of the Euro-Atlantic community. In light of the challenges and opportunities posed by the AKP's approach to foreign affairs, the key foreign policy test for Turkey and its Western allies in coming years will be to insulate their 50-year partnership from the strains posed by some of the AKP's Islamist convictions and ambitions.

CHAPTER SIX

Looking Ahead: Will Islamism Replace Kemalism?

To recapitulate, for centuries, Islam and the West have been competing to define Turkish identity. In 1923, when Atatürk founded the Turkish Republic, he established legal and governmental mechanisms to allow Turks to embrace Islam in their private lives while restraining religion from public affairs. Atatürk's determination to separate mosque and state sprang from his belief that the fledgling republic needed to modernize if it were to survive. He believed that modernization would require dramatic reforms through which Turkey would both *adopt* and *adapt to* Europe's technological and societal advances since the Renaissance. The Ottomans had permitted Europe to bypass their empire due to what Atatürk viewed as close-mindedness resulting from a narrow interpretation of Islam that prevailed under Ottoman rule. Atatürk's modern republic would be anchored in the West but based on the Turkic heritage of the East; democracy and Islam would coexist, but public life would be governed by modern secular laws rather than *sharia*.

Following Atatürk's death, Islam episodically regained momentum as an important factor in Turkish identity, but was held in check by civilian and military officials who considered themselves the custodians of Turkey's secular democracy. On four occasions, the military ousted Turkey's civilian governments. Each time, the military returned political authority to Turkey's civilian leaders relatively quickly. The model of democracy that governs the republic has thus been peculiar and tumultuous, yet vibrant.

During the past four decades, those who have sought to soften the boundary between Islam and public life have become more organized and influential in Turkish politics. Beginning in the 1970s, Fethullah Gülen's movement and Necmettin Erbakan's Islamist political parties launched grassroots efforts to restore Islam's key role. In practice, this has meant nudging Turks to accept elements of *sharia* in both private and public life.

Increasing evidence suggests that AKP leaders, many of whom began their political careers within Erbakan's organizations, are now building on his Islamist legacy and using state institutions to shape public opinion in favor of Islamism. Secularists point to sharp increases in the number of state religious schools and the introduction of Islamic practices there as clear indicators of a troubling shift. Statistics showing declines in gender equality and respect for religious and ethnic minorities seem to corroborate the Kemalists' fears about the erosion of the boundary between religion and public life—

and with it, the weakening of secular democracy. Such statistics counter the AKP's insistence that it is simply implementing reforms and other domestic policies that reflect the will of the Turkish voters.

A shift also appears to be underway in Turkish foreign policy, as Europe and the United States ebb in Ankara's national-security calculations and Turkey's neighbors rise in importance. Here many factors are at work. The end of the Cold War obviated Turkey's mission as the defender of NATO's southern flank, and offered Ankara fresh opportunities to develop relations with new states whose Turkic populations gained independence from the Soviet Union. Some degree of deterioration in Turkey's relations with the West was perhaps inevitable, after the United States proceeded with its war in Iraq and when key European leaders seemed to retreat from the EU's commitment to accept Turkey as a full member if Ankara implemented necessary reforms. After all, nationalism is the one political factor that transcends all Turkish political divisions.

But the intensity of the AKP government's anti-U.S. vitriol in 2003–04 and its harsh criticism of Israel in 2009 suggest that an appeal to pan-Islamism may now rival considerations of realpolitik in determining Turkish foreign policy. Ankara's embrace of Islamist regimes in Sudan, Gaza, and Iran provide further evidence of the growing importance of Islamist ideology in determining Turkey's approach to the world.

Turkey's voters will, in the end, determine whether "Islamism at home, pan-Islamism in the world" eventually replaces Atatürk's adage of "peace at home, peace in the world." For now, the electorate is reacting cautiously to such a momentous change; the public overwhelmingly favors retention of Turkey's secular and democratic system while embracing Turkic traditions, including Islam, in the private sphere. In foreign policy, neither the AKP's supporters nor those of its opponents seek to abandon Turkey's partnership with the Euro-Atlantic community. Yes, there is a national consensus—and resentment—that the West under-appreciates Turkey's strategic importance and that Europe views Turkey as too big and too Muslim to be accepted as a full EU member. But the Turks continue to recognize that political self-interest make NATO, the EU, and the United States their critical allies.

Still, Turkish domestic politics and foreign policy are evolving in new directions. The AKP is operating from a position of strength as it strives to restore Islam as a key determinant of the Turkish identity. For the first time since 1923, those who seek to soften Atatürk's barrier between Islam and public life have secured the key positions of state power the Kemalists relied on to protect secularism—e.g., the presidency, parliament, prime ministry, courts, ministry of internal affairs, and university rectors. The AKP also enjoys increasing influence over media outlets through its control of state broadcasters and its alliances with powerful figures who now own major newspapers and television stations. The Ergenekon investigation has intimidated journalists business and civil society leaders, and senior military officers into silence, and the enormous tax penalty against the Doğan Media Group could eliminate the AKP's most powerful potential challenger in the media world. Meanwhile, the AKP's secular opponents have failed to find a message that appeals to mainstream voters.

For all the electoral success of the Islamists, Turkey's political majority lies in the conservative center, and has grown weary of Islamist-secularist tension. The mainstream political desire for a stable democracy that embraces both secularism in government and Islam in private life was captured by the slogan embraced by millions of demonstrators in mid-2007: "no *sharia*, no coup." Such sentiment was also reflected in the results of Turkey's municipal elections in March 2009. Prime Minister Erdoğan originally predicted that the AKP would win 50 percent of the vote, then adjusted his target to 40 percent as the AKP dropped in the polls. In the end, the AKP fell just below even that revised goal. In Antalya and Izmir, where the AKP campaigned most actively through repeated appearances by Erdoğan (and threatened to cut the budgets of municipalities if non-AKP candidates were elected), voters nonetheless rejected the party's candidates. And polls in February 2010 indicated AKP support at around 30 percent.

In coming months, the AKP and its Kemalist opponents will probably sharpen their political battle lines. Whether this political struggle will shake the majority of Turkish voters from their current conservative preference for secular democracy and private embrace of Islam will depend on whether the AKP can deepen and sustain its hold on power. For now, the ruling party seems intent on bolstering its domestic political position by silencing its critics and expanding its control over media outlets. Although those are crude tactics, if they succeed, the

AKP's potential challengers will face even greater difficulty unseating it. To do so, they will have to mount a successful appeal to the large mass of voters in Turkey's political center. As of this writing, the AKP government has proposed amending Turkey's constitution to "strengthen democracy" in accordance with EU accession requirements. How this debate plays out will likely determine whether the AKP will push for further constitutional reforms that could more seriously weaken the tenets of secularism and elevate the social role of Islam. (The result may be a hardening of anti-Turkey sentiments within the EU, a price the AKP may be willing to pay.)

On the other hand, an over-confident AKP may overstep its popularity. Many centrists in Turkish politics are already criticizing what they view as the party's increasingly authoritarian tendencies, which they fear are undermining democracy. There are limits to how much backsliding on fundamental freedoms non-Islamist Turks will tolerate. Voters may rebel against growing restrictions on freedom of expression; more women may reject the deterioration in gender equality since 2002 and the growing effort to define their social identity by Islamic norms; and members of religious minorities may form a critical mass of political opposition to anti-Semitism and anti-Alevi discrimination they believe AKP is fomenting. But as of early 2010, Turkey's voices of protest remain relatively quiet.

In the AKP's relations with one important constituency, senior military leaders, Prime Minister Erdoğan seemed intent on maintaining this political quietness, as throughout 2009 he built a cooperative personal relationship with the current chief of the general staff, İlker Basbuğ. That strategy was in grave danger of being shattered in late February of this year, when nearly 50 current and former military officers, including three of the country's highest-ranking ex-generals were arrested on charges of plotting a coup in 2003. (Several of these had worked closely with the AKP government against Turkey's top national security threat, PKK terrorism, and achieved dramatic success through trilateral cooperation among Turkey, the United States, and Iraq.)

In foreign policy, the AKP is defying the United States and its European Allies on the issue of Iran at the United Nations. Ankara may soon face a defining moment in its relations with the West: the United States and its EU allies are preparing a new round of sanctions against Tehran for its continued nuclear weapons programs. Turkey has opposed further sanctions; will it continue do so as the betting in this international poker game continues to mount?

Ankara is also defying Washington and several of its key Western Allies with regard to Israel, reflecting anti-Israel and anti-American sentiment the AKP has both harnessed and catalyzed in Turkish society. AKP leaders regularly condemn their Israeli counterparts for "war crimes" in Gaza, but make little or no mention of Palestinian attacks on Israelis. The AKP's embrace of (Islamist) Hamas and rejection of (secular) Fatah trumpets a tilt toward Islamism; but the Kemalists hesitate to buck a policy that resonates with Turkey's general public. Ankara's anti-Israel and pro-Hamas approach will continue unless and until leaders across Turkey's political spectrum realize that this approach jeopardizes Ankara's ability to act as an honest broker in discussions between Israel and Syria. Moreover, the longer Ankara pursues these policies, the further it moves away from the West, and the harder it will be for Turkey to get back on track with its Euro-Atlantic allies.

The AKP's reluctance to pressure Iran and Hamas will continue to generate tension between Ankara and the rest of the Euro-Atlantic alliance. The European Union can help temper Turkey's pugnacious approach to the Middle East if key European leaders drop their expressed preference for Turkey to receive only a "privileged partnership"—even if Ankara implements the complete program of mandated reforms—rather than full EU membership. But getting EU-Turkish relations fully on track will also require the AKP to make those reforms and to facilitate a Cyprus settlement. Achieving these goals, in turn, will require clearer leadership from the AKP that Turkey's strategic home lies within the Euro-Atlantic community and anchored in NATO and the EU, rather than between East and West and tethered to the Organization of the Islamic Conference (OIC).

Finally, Turkey's relations with the United States will have a major impact on Ankara's approach to the world. If Turkey and the United States can sustain a broad sense of partnership, Ankara will retain Euro-Atlanticism as a fundamental strategic policy and a tool for building its political support at home. But sustaining an American-Turkish partnership will be more difficult if Ankara decides to cooperate with Washington only on some issues (e.g., Afghanistan/Pakistan, Iraq) while preferring to partner with Russia and/or Islamist regimes on others (e.g., Iran, the Caucasus, energy security).

For decades, U.S. foreign policy has assumed that Turkey can exist simultaneously as a key member *of* the West and as a strategic bridge *between* East and West. In the wake of the terrorist attacks of September 11, 2001, Washington hoped the AKP might emerge as the Islamic equivalent of Europe's Christian democratic parties. The Pax Americana in the broader Middle East needed a positive model of a successful and tolerant Muslim state at peace with the world, and Turkey came close to answering that need.

Some of that hope has faded in Washington, as anti-Americanism lingered beyond the presidency of George W. Bush. The durability of anti-Americanism in Turkey suggests that a deep realignment may be occurring within Turkish society. The next few years will be decisive in determining whether it actually occurs, as Turkish voters ponder whether to preserve, refresh, or replace the secular democratic system that has defined their national identity since 1923. At the forefront of such deliberations will be the debate that has endured in Turkey for decades: should Islam dominate social life or be confined to the privacy of the individual believer?

In the mid-'90s novel *The New Life*, a canonical work by Turkey's Nobel Laureate, Orhan Pamuk, a young student (appropriately named Osman, as in the founder of the Ottoman Empire) embarks on a voyage of discovery of his own country. After he had read a book, which unsettled and changed him, Osman abandons his studies, turns his back on his family, "gets on buses, and off buses," loiters in bus terminals, embarks and disembarks in small towns, and goes deep into the arid Anatolian heartland. He encounters dreamers and entrepreneurs, peasants and state officials, ordinary people devoted both to Atatürk's statue in the local square and to the mosque next door.

Toward the end of his wanderings, in a forlorn town, an avuncular candyman, offers him a free piece of mint candy, along with ruminations on the world. "Today we are altogether defeated," the candyman says. "The West has swallowed us up, trampled on us in passing. They have invaded us down to our soup, our candy, our underpants; they have finished us off. But someday, someday perhaps a thousand years from now, we will avenge ourselves; we will bring an end to this conspiracy by taking them out of our soup, our chewing gum, and our souls. Now go ahead and eat your mints, don't cry over spilt milk."

By the standards of their Muslim neighbors in Iran and the Arab lands, the Turks are remarkably resilient and somewhat averse to crying over "spilt milk." They have a history of success that is reflected in their current position in the world. But they have resisted the siren song of historical revenge and the dreams of imperial restoration. Their leading foreign historian, Bernard Lewis, once described the Turks as the most "earnest" of Islam's peoples. Perhaps it is that earnestness that may yet temper the intense struggle between secularists and Islamists, in their most recent battle over Turkey's destination.

NOTES

Introduction: Turkey's Choice

1. The Pew Global Attitudes Project, *Confidence in Obama Lifts U.S. Image Around the World: Most Muslim Publics Not So Easily Moved*, July 2009; pewglobal .org/reports/display.php?ReportID = 264 (accessed October 12, 2009).

2. The German Marshall Fund of the United States, *Transatlantic Trends: Key Findings 2009* (Washington, D.C.: The German Marshall Fund of the United States, September 2009), 26.

3. The Pew Global Attitudes Project, *America's Image Slips, But Allies Share U.S. Concerns over Iran, Hamas*, June 2006; pewglobal.org/reports/pdf/252.pdf (accessed October 14, 2009).

4. Samuel Huntington, *The Clash of Civilizations and the Remaking of World Order* (New York: Simon and Schuster, 1998).

5. The Pew Global Attitudes Project, *World Public Welcomes Global Trade—But Not Immigration*, October 4, 2007; pewglobal.org/reports/pdf/258.pdf (accessed October 14, 2009).

6. Turkish Economic and Social Studies Foundation, *Religion, Society and Politics in Contemporary Turkey* (Istanbul: Turkish Economic and Social Studies Foundation, November 2006), 7.

Chapter One: Turkish Identity— from the Ottomans to Atatürk

1. Ottoman historian Bernard Lewis argues, however, that the Ottomans did not employ this title until the late eighteenth century, when they used the Caliphate to counter the Russians.

2. Norman Itzkowitz, "The Ottoman Empire," in Bernard Lewis, ed., *The World of Islam* (London: Thames and Hudson, 1976), 277.

3. Niyazi Berkes, *Türkiye'de Çağdaşlaşma* (Modernization in Turkey) (Istanbul: Yapı Kredi Yayınları, 2002), 27.

4. Sobieski's forces are believed to have begun the attacks on September 11.

5. Bernard Lewis, *What Went Wrong: The Clash Between Islam and Modernity in the Middle East* (New York: Oxford University Press, 2002), 18.

6. *What Went Wrong*, 20–34.

7. *Türkiye'de Çağdaşlaşma*, 328–42.

8. Francois Georgeon, *Osmanlı-Türk Modernleşmesi* (Ottoman-Turkish Modernization): *1900–1930*, translated into Turkish from French by Ali Berktay (Istanbul: Yapı Kredi Yayınları, 2000), 3.

9. *Osmanlı-Türk Modernleşmesi*, 4.

10. *Türkiye'de Çağdaşlaşma*, 527–36.

Chapter Two: The Rise of Political Islam and the AKP

1. Şerif Mardin, *Türkiye'de din ve siyaset* (Religion and Politics in Turkey) (Istanbul: İletişim, 1991), 170–93.

2. Ruşen Çakir, *İmam Hatip Liseleri: Efsaneler ve Gerçekler* (İmam Hatip Schools: Myths and Facts) (Istanbul: Turkish Economic and Social Studies Foundation, October 2004), 60–7.

3. *Radikal*, "Kanli konuşma için ağır tahrik savunması" (Bloody Speech in Response to Provocation), August 10, 2000; www.radikal.com.tr/2000/08/10/politika/kan.shtml (accessed November 2, 2009).

4. Although the number of İmam Hatip students increased during Erbakan's term, it decreased by half when the next administration took over.

5. The D-8 members are Turkey, Iran, Indonesia, Malaysia, Egypt, Pakistan, Bangladesh, and Nigeria.

6. Stephen Kinzer, "Turkey Secularists Take Their Battle into Court," *The New York Times*, April 5, 1998, 16; www.nytimes.com/1998/04/05/world/turkey-secularists-take-their-battle-into-court.html?sec = &spon = &partner = permalink&exprod; eqpermalink (accessed November 7, 2009).

Chapter Three: The AKP's Political Victories

1. Ömer Dinçer, "21.Yüzyıla Girerken Dünya ve Türkiye Gündeminde İslam" (Islam in the Global and the Turkish Agenda in the Wake of the Twenty-

First Century), *Bilgi ve Hikmet* (Knowledge and Wisdom), No. 12, 1995 3–7; *also see* Sedat Ergin, "Başbakanlık Müsteşarı Siyasal İslamcı Olunca" (When Undersecretary of Prime Ministry is a Political Islamist), *Hürriyet*, December 28, 2003; arama.hurriyet.com.tr/arsivnews.aspx?id = 192432 (accessed November 7, 2009).

2. Erdoğan said (translation of sentences in text), "Mahkemenin de bu konuda söz söyleme hakkı yoktur. Söz söyleme hakkı din ulemasınındır." İrfan Kurtulmuş, "Erdoğan Doktrini" (Erdoğan Doctrine), *Milliyet*, November 16, 2005; www.milliyet.com.tr/2005/11/16/siyaset/asiy/html (accessed November 8, 2009).

3. *Yeni Şafak*, "Laiklik sosyal hayatı cezaevine çevirmemeli" (Secularism Should Not Turn Life into a Prison), April 26, 2006; yenisafak.com.tr/Arsiv/2006/Nisan/26/g01.html (accessed November 9, 2009).

4. *Radikal*, "Arınç: 'Cumhurbaşkani Sivil ve Dindar Olacak'" (Arınç: "There Will Be a Civilian and Religious President"), April 16, 2007; www.radikal.com.tr/haber.php?haberno = 218512 (accessed November 9, 2009).

5. The Constitutional Court closed the DTP on December 11, 2009, acting on the Supreme Court of Appeals chief prosecutor's charges, in November 2007, that the party was encouraging violence and cooperating with the PKK.

6. In a referendum in October 2007, Turks decided to elect their next president directly, instead of continuing with parliamentary election. The next presidential elections are in 2012.

7. Soner Yalçın, "AKP'nin tesettüre girme hikayeleri" (Stories of AKP [leaders' wives and daughters] donning the veil), *Hürriyet*, February 10, 2008; arama.hurriyet.com.tr/arsivnews.aspx?id = 8201591 (accessed November 13, 2009).

8. Sabrina Tavernise and Şebnem Arsu, "Turkish Court Calls Ruling Party Constitutional," *The New York Times,* July 31, 2008; www.nytimes.com/2008/07/31/world/europe/31turkey.html?_r = 1 (accessed November 13, 2009).

Chapter Four: Reshaping Identity by Restoring Islam

1. Ali Sevim, Akif Tural, and İzzet Öztoprak, eds., *Atatürk'ün Söylev ve Demeçleri* (Atatürk's Speeches and Statements), Vol. II. (Ankara: Türk Inkilap Tarihi Enstitüsü Yayinlari, 1959).

2. Kemal Karpat, *Social Change and Politics in Turkey: A Structural-Historical Analysis* (Lciden, The Netherlands: E.J. Brill, 1973).

3. Hüseyin Özalp, "Rakibimiz Uzan" (Our Competitor is Uzan), *Sabah,* June 4, 2003; arsiv.sabah.com.tr/2003/06/04/p01.html (accessed February 18, 2010).

4. *NTVMSNBC,* "Yıldırım: Dinlenmek istemeyen konuşmasin" (Those who do not want to be eavesdropped on should not talk [on the phone]) January 29, 2009; arsiv.ntvmsnbc.com/news/473678.asp (accessed November 17, 2009).

5. *Milliyet,* "Baykal: Bir korku toplumu yaratılıyor" (Baykal: A society of fear is being created), July 3, 2008; www.milliyet.com.tr/default.aspx?aType = Haber Detay&ArticleID = 889322 (accessed November 17, 2009).

6. Her funeral took place on May 19, the same day Atatürk stepped foot in Samsun and began the War of Liberation.

7. *Hürriyet,* "Baykal: 'Tarikat dışında eğitim suç haline geldi' " (Baykal: Education that is not provided by religious orders has become a crime), April 16, 2009; www.hurriyet.com.tr/gundem/11442297.asp (accessed November 23, 2009).

8. "Gulen movement: Turkey's third power," *Jane's Islamic Affairs Analyst,* January 29, 2009; jiaa.janes.com/public/jiaa/index.shtml (accessed November 23, 2009).

9. Binnaz Toprak, İrfan Bozan, Tan Morgül, and Nedim Şener, *Türkiye'de farklı olmak: din ve muhafazakarlık ekseninde ötekileştirilenler* (Being Different in Turkey: Becoming the Others on the Axis of Religion and Conservatism) (Istanbul: Boğaziçi Üniversitesi, 2008), 145–6.

10. Okan Konuralp, "Kuran Kursuna Rağbet Katlandı" (Interest in the Qur'an Schools Multiplied), *Hürriyet,* April 4, 2008; www.hurriyet.com.tr/gundem/8589945.asp (accessed November 28, 2009).

11. Angel Rabasa and Stephen Larrabee, *The Rise of Political Islam in Turkey* (Washington, D.C.: The RAND Corporation, 2008), 19.

12. Betül Kotan, "Dersimiz felsefeden çıkış" (Our Lesson: Departing Philosophy), *Radikal,* October 3, 2008; www.radikal.com.tr/Default.aspx?aType = HaberDetay&ArticleID = 901479&Date = 03.10.2008&CategoryID = 97 (accessed December 4, 2009).

13. As cited in Mark Kaufman, "In Turkey, fertile ground for creationism," *The Washington Post,* November 8, 2009; www.washingtonpost.com/wp-dyn/content/article/2009/11/07/AR2009110702233.html (accessed December 8, 2009).

14. *Spiegel Online,* "Turkey's Catalog of Sins: Religious Authority Warns Women against Perfume, Flirtation," May 29, 2008; www.spiegel.de/international/world/0,1518,556262,00.html (accessed November 15, 2009).

15. *Milliyet,* "*Diyanet* Vakfı'ndan Şaşırtan Kitaplar" (Surprising Books from the Diyanet Foundation), September 26, 2007; www.milliyet.com.tr/2007/09/26/son/sontur32.asp (accessed November 15, 2009).

16. Yeşim Arat, *Religion, Politics and Gender Equality in Turkey: Implications of a Democratic Paradox* (Geneva: The United Nations Research Institute for Social Development, September 2009), 3.

17. Yalçin, "*AKP'nin tesettüre* girme hikayeleri," February 10, 2008.

18. Gülay Atasoy. "How Did They Come to Cover Themselves?" cited in "AKP'nin tesettüre girme hikayeleri," February 10, 2008.

19. "Social and Economic Benefits of More and Better Job Opportunities for Women in Turkey," Executive Summary, World Bank and State Planning Organization of Turkey, September 15, 2009; www.worldbank.org.tr/WBSITE/EXTERNAL/COUNTRIES/ECAEXT/TURKEYEXTN/0,,print:Y~isCURL:Y~contentMDK:22313638~pagePK:1497618~piPK:217854~theSitePK:361712,00.html (accessed December 3, 2009).

20. Turkish Enterprise and Business Confederation. *İş Dünyasında Kadın* (Women in the Business World) (Istanbul: Artpress, December 2007), 24–5; www.turkonfed.org/rapor/isdunyasindakadin.pdf (accessed December 3, 2009).

21. Government of Turkey, United Nations Development Programme, *Women in Politics,* 2007, 3; www.undp.org.tr/demGovDocs/Signed%20Project%20Document%20-%20Women%20in%20Politics%20-%2000049635.pdf (accessed December 3, 2009).

22. CNN Türk, "Bakan Şimşek işsizliğin neden arttığını açıkladı" (Finance Minister Şimşek explained why unemployment increased), March 18, 2009; www.cnnturk.com/2009/ekonomi/genel/03/18/bakan.simsek.issizligin.neden.arttigini.acikladi/518347.0/index.html (accessed December 11, 2009).

23. Tarik Işik, "Yapma Diyanet, Etme Diyanet" (Don't Do This, Diyanet), *Radikal,* May 27, 2008; www.radikal.com.tr/Default.aspx?aType = Detay&ArticleID = 879903&Date = 27.05.2008&CategoryID = 77 (accessed December 11, 2009). See also *Spiegel Online,* "Turkey's Catalog of Sins: Religious Authority Warns Women against Perfume, Flirtation," May 29, 2008; www.spiegel.de/international/world/0,1518,556262,00.html. (accessed December 11, 2009).

24. Soner Çağaptay, "A Trap for Muslims," *Hürriyet Daily News,* October 25, 2009; www.hurriyetdailynews.com/n.php?n = a-trap-for-muslims-2009-10-24 (accessed October 29, 2009).

25. The Pew Global Attitudes Project, *Unfavorable Views of Jews and Muslims on the Increase in Europe* (Washington, D.C.: Pew Research Center, September 2008), 10.

26. Leyla Navaro, "Türkiye'de Yahudi olmak: 500 yıllık yalnızlık" (Being Jewish in Turkey: a 500-year-old solitude), *Radikal*, January 22, 2009; www.radi kal.com.tr/Radikal.aspx?aType = RadikalHaberDetay&ArticleID = 918064& Date = 23.01.2009&CategoryID = 99 (accessed December 2, 2009).

27. *Radikal*, "İçki satan noktalar hizla azalıyor" (Places that sell alcohol are diminishing fast), September 12, 2008; www.radikal.com.tr/Default.aspx?aType = HaberDetay&ArticleID = 898241&Date = 12.09.2008&CategoryID = 97 (accessed November 17, 2009).

28. Nuray Başaran, "AK Partili Tuğcu: Devletten iş almak isteyen müteahhidin eşinin örtünmesi şansını yükseltir" (AK Party Member Tuğcu: If a contractor's wife wears a headscarf, his chances of winning government contracts will be increased), *Referans*, September 21, 2007; www.referansgazetesi.com/haber .aspx?HBR_KOD = 78737&ForArsiv = 1 (accessed February 18, 2010).

Chapter Five: The AKP's Foreign Policy

1. On the question "Is Turkey turning away from the West?" see Dan Bilefsky, "Tensions Between Turkey and the West Increase," *The New York Times*, October 27, 2009, A12; Robert Tait, "Turkish PM exposes nuclear rift in NATO," *The Guardian*, October 26, 2009, www.guardian.co.uk/world/2009/oct/ 26/turkey-iran (accessed December 14, 2009); *The Christian Science Monitor*, "Turkey's worrisome approach to Iran, Israel," October 29, 2009, www.csmoni tor.com/Commentary/the-monitors-view/2009/1029/p08s01-comv.html (accessed December 14, 2009); and Soner Çağaptay, "Is Turkey Leaving the West," *Foreign Affairs Online*, October 26, 2009, www.foreignaffairs.com/articles/ 65634/soner-cagaptay/is-turkey-leaving-the-west-?page = 2 (accessed December 14, 2009).

2. Ahmet Davutoğlu, *Stratejik Derinlik: Türkiye'nin Uluslararasi Konumu* (Strategic Depth: Turkey's International Position) (Istanbul: Küre Yayinlari, 2001).

3. Katrin Bennhold, "Leaders of Turkey and Israel Clash at Davos Panel," *New York Times,* January 29, 2009, A6.

4. *Radikal*, "Erdoğan: Bati'nın ahlaksızlığını aldık," January 25, 2008; www .radikal.com.tr/haber.php?haberno = 245471 (accessed December 14, 2010).

5. Re Erdoğan's full remarks on assimilation being a "crime against humanity," see *Spiegel Online*, "Erdoğan's Visit Leaves German Conservatives Fuming," February 12, 2008; www.spiegel.de/international/germany/0,1518,534724,00 .html (accessed December 14, 2009).

6. Deputy Secretary of Defense Wolfowitz, interview with CNN *Türk*, May 2003; www.defense.gov/Transcripts/Transcript.aspx?TranscriptID = 2572 (accessed December 14, 2009).

7. Re Bush's pledge to cooperate with Turkey against the PKK, see "Remarks Following a Meeting with Prime Minister Recep Tayyip Erdoğan of Turkey and an Exchange With Reporters," 2007 Presidential Documents Online via GOP Access," November 5, 2007; frwebgate6.access.gpo.gov/cgi-bin/TEXT gate.cgi?WAISdocID = 989532493153 + 0 + 1 + 0&WAISaction = retrieve (accessed December 14, 2009).

ABOUT THE AUTHOR

ZEYNO BARAN is senior fellow and director of the Center for Eurasian Policy at the Hudson Institute and an associate scholar at its Center on Islam, Democracy and the Future of the Muslim World. She previously directed the International Security and Energy Programs at the Nixon Center; before that she directed the Georgia Forum and the Caucasus Project at the Center for Strategic and International Studies.

Her current work focuses on strategies to thwart the spread of radical Islamist ideology in Europe and in Eurasia and to promote reform across Eurasia. Her most recent book is *The Other Muslims: Moderate and Secular* (Palgrave, March 2010).

Born in Istanbul, Turkey, and raised partly in Athens, Greece, Baran received her BA in international economic development and her BA in political science from Stanford University.

Herbert and Jane Dwight
Working Group on
Islamism and the
International Order

The Herbert and Jane Dwight Working Group on Islamism and the International Order seeks to engage in the task of reversing Islamic radicalism through reforming and strengthening the legitimate role of the state across the entire Muslim world. Efforts will draw on the intellectual resources of an array of scholars and practitioners from within the United States and abroad, to foster the pursuit of modernity, human flourishing, and the rule of law and reason in Islamic lands—developments that are critical to the very order of the international system.

The Working Group is chaired by Hoover fellows Fouad Ajami and Charles Hill with an active participation of Director John Raisian. Current core membership includes Russell A. Berman, Abbas Milani, and Shelby Steele, with contributions from Zeyno Baran, Reuel Marc Gerecht, Ziad Haider, John Hughes, Nibras Kazimi, Habib Malik, and Joshua Teitelbaum.

INDEX

Abbas, Mahmoud, 121
Abdülhamit II (sultan of Ottoman
    Empire), 19–21, 30
Abdullah (king of Saudi Arabia), 122
Abdülmecit II (sultan of Ottoman
    Empire), 18
Abu Ghraib prison, 131
administrative law. *See kanun*
Afghanistan, 14, 36, 124
Ahmadinejad, Mahmud, 122
Ajami, Fouad, xv
Akman, Zahid, 77
AKP (Justice and Development Party)
    2002 electoral victory for, 2–3, 34,
        50–51, 129–130
    2007 elections for, 60–67
    2009 municipal elections for, 8,
        143
    closing down, Ergenekon case for,
        68–70, 79–82
    democratic image strategy of,
        53–54
    economic record of, 65–66
    Erbakan's influence on, 46, 47, 51
    foreign policy under, 105–106,
        116–137, 145–147

future strategies for, 143–144
gender (in)equality under, 91–96
Gül as candidate for, 61, 62, 64, 67
Iraq War and, 127–133
Islamist education promotion by,
    86–88
Islamist roots and agenda of, 3–4,
    7, 44–45, 55–57, 140–141
media control by, 75–78, 82–84,
    142
military role and authority *vs.*, 54,
    59–60, 62
overview, 57–58, 101–102
platform strategy, 46–48
protest rallies against, 64–65
rise of, 44–45, 46–51
Sezer's secular counterattack to,
    58–59
supporters of, 8, 63, 74, 147
See also Erdoğan, Recep Tayyip;
    Gül, Abdullah
Albayrak, Berat, 76, 83
alcohol consumption, 98, 99–100
Alevis, 10, 40, 48, 98–99
Aliyev, Heydar, 114

161